EXPANDING INTO THE LIGHT:

Discovering the Realms of Near Death Experiences Through
Spiritual Practices

Ron Jones, Ph.D.

Published by FastPencil

Published by FastPencil
307 Orchard City Drive
Suite 210
Campbell CA 95008 USA
info@fastpencil.com
(408) 540-7571
(408) 540-7572 (Fax)
http://www.fastpencil.com

Printed in the United States of America.

Third Edition

I dedicate this to the seekers on all spiritual paths.

ॐ

Acknowledgments

So many people supported this work in various ways. I don't know how to properly thank my magical wife, Sharyn (whose magical energy regularly messes up her electronic devices) for sharing her NDE with me so openly, and now for sharing it with the world through this project. She gave me encouragement, time and suggestions along the way to make this book happen. She is my soul mate and my partner in "Liquid Love".

I want to thank others who read and edited the book before publication: Thank you to Sheila, Nancy and others in my "Sadhana Circle" at the meditation center who consistently helped the flow and content of the book. Thank you to my daughter Rebecca who was helpful in chapter placement and other edits. Thank you to my best friend Errol for his suggestions in making the exercises in the last chapters of the book more accessible to the reader. A special thank you to my cousin Jenny, who discovered with me that we had a mutual interest in the spiritual realm and who not only offered editing advice, but also created the reference pages for me with her experiences as a university librarian. A very special thank you goes to Fran Hopkins whom I met on a trip to Turkey. We learned that we could each help the other out with our analytic skills and traded our reviewing efforts on each others projects!

The most significant thank you is to my Gurus and all my prior meditation teachers, including Anne and Jim Armstrong, without whose spiritual guidance this book would not exist. Thank you, thank you, thank you. Om Shanti Shanti Shanti.

Contents

PART I - EXPERIENCES OF THE LIGHT

THE LIGHT
AS DISCOVERED THROUGH
NEAR DEATH EXPERIENCES AND MEDITATION

The Transforming Event

I STARTED FORMULATING THE content of this book during a period when my wife, Sharyn, and I were comparing spiritual experiences. Our experiences emanated from different spiritual journeys in each case, hers through a near death experience (NDE) and mine through the path of yoga meditation, yet we both awakened to the same absolute wonder in reaction to the higher realms of human experience. We both experienced our innate nature as pure intelligent light, pure joy, pure love and, ultimately, as pure awareness itself. There was a deep validation of higher reality for both of us in our separate journeys. After some years of intermittently sharing different aspects of our experiences, I realized I wanted to capture the essence of those similarities of experience and build on them to explore the world that exists deeply within each of us. For both of us our experiences are considered spiritually transforming experiences, STEs, and our lives have not been the same following them.

The incapacitated body in a near-death experience might make that experience one of the more complete absorptions into divine light, for the very reason that the body is in fact completely switched off and therefore stilled. On the other hand, meditation, chanting and prayer are of such extreme value because they create the conditions of stillness and focus necessary for us to transcend the body and experience the divine light without dying. **It is my conviction that NDErs and committed meditaters can learn a tremendous amount from each other.** The purity of NDE experiences can inform and inspire meditaters, while experienced meditaters stand as examples for NDErs that one can soar in the light without trauma or clinical death. My writings might also motivate yet another group, those who have a growing interest in life's mysteries but haven't so far had an experience of them. Both NDE and meditation experiences probably hold something useful for most seekers. I would hope therefore that the topics covered in this book will inspire a wide range of people.

I am an advisor to The American Center for the Integration of Spiritually Transformative Experiences (aciste.org), an organization formed to broaden the group of experiences of heavenly realms and the Light of Consciousness to include all sources, including but not limited to NDEs. However, since my wife's experience was in fact an NDE, I do focus on that catalyst for the shift to dimensions of light that she experienced. My meditation experiences, though, are a good example of the need for the designation STE that is at the core of establishing ACISTE; these experiences were achieved without dying (unless ego death is included as an NDE!).

Sharyn told me about her first experience of "The Light" one evening after we had seen the movie *Flatliners* that included Hollywood images of crossing over to the other side of everyday reality. Our first commitment ceremony to each other in 1987 was in an Ashram and was unexpectedly powerful and spiritually moving. It definitely connected our hearts and cemented our relationship to one another. The Spiritual Master who married us literally tied a knot in the shawl wrapped around the two of us together, not so subtly demonstrating that we had "Tied The Knot". We designed the second wedding ceremony in 1989 to be more digestible by relatives and friends, though we did include some unusual aspects to the ceremony to make it uniquely ours. I sang to Sharyn as she walked down the aisle and again during the ceremony. Also, unbeknown to her, I asked a friend of ours to jump up and object when we came to that part of the ceremony, shocking everyone present with a comedy routine of outrage at my negative influence on her perfectly fine life!

Sharyn and I obviously knew about our spiritual connection. We had even attended meditation intensives and retreats together. However, after seeing *Flatliners*, we were both tearing-up and felt like we were soaring in space with the angelic souls depicted in that movie. We talked for hours about our experiences soaring in "The Light" and I knew then that I had to write about the similarities that were so exciting to us that night.

Sharyn cannot remember her NDE without emotion. She says it was the most powerful, painful, yet loving experience, she has ever had. It happened at a time when she was not seeking anything, not thinking about religion or spiritual matters, nor needing anything special in her life. She was attending Stagg High School in Stockton California. She was an extroverted 16 year old girl, loving her senior year, excited by her many school activities, enjoying her friends and active social life, and delighted with the success she was having with one of her favorite high school interests — drama. It was January 6, 1959 and she was trying out for the senior play with several of her close friends. She had a thrilling night because she read for the part of Dorothy in *The Wizard of Oz*. It was one of her favorite productions and she adored and identified with Judy Garland in the movie.

She did not realize that she would soon be embarking on a spiritual trip down her own yellow brick road!

Sharyn had just found out she had been cast as Dorothy, and she was ecstatic about it. Since it was a cold and drizzly night, she and several of her cast mates were driven home by her drama instructor, Mr. "L.". Sharyn was bubbly and talkative all the way home, eager to tell her mother about the part for which she had been chosen. She knew both parents would be pleased since they both had been involved in the theater arts, her father was a business manager at one time for Mae West, Ginger Rogers, Elaine Barrymore and others and her mother directed the Miss California Pageant and local theater performances for many years.

Mr. "L.". let her off just across the street from her home. Through the rain, Sharyn could see that the front porch light was on. Although she knew her father was not home, she knew her mother would be there. To avoid getting wet, she quickly got out, looked in both directions, and then ran behind Mr. "L."'s car and into the street toward her house, buoyed by her exciting news. However, as she moved across the mid-line of the street she noticed to her right a light bouncing off the fender of a fast-approaching car. It was driven, she would later learn, by a drunk driver. Even though she only had a couple of seconds to react, she remembers things slowing down so she had time to mentally prepare - not just for the accident, but its possible consequences. She remembers thinking calmly that she would probably die. The impact threw her into the air, and dropped her broken body many feet down the road.

The accident affected Sharyn in opposing ways: It is hard to imagine anything more painful, confining, socially debilitating, and frustrating than the kind of brutal assault that breaks up a human body like so many dry twigs. However, at the same time, the accident immediately thrust her into what she ranks as one of the most rapturous, loving and life transforming experiences of her life - a near-death-experience. Although the term "Near Death Experience" (NDE) had not yet been coined, Sharyn's experience fit the classic description later published in Dr. Raymond Moody's book, *Life After Life*. Dr. Moody extensively studied and wrote about people's experiences of being clinically or nearly dead before reawakening to the world. For Sharyn, as with other NDErs, it was a profoundly spiritual event that changed the entire direction and understanding of her life.

An interesting side note is that Sharyn was given Dr. Raymond Moody's book when her dad was in the hospital after he suffered a stroke toward the end of his life. The book had just come out. She had not heard of it, but a social worker at the hospital gave it to her to read as preparation for the possibility her dad might not survive. She discovered while reading it that she was not the only one to have had a NDE! She wonders if it was synchronistically placed in her hands so she could better understand her own experience.

Medically speaking, Sharyn's pelvis had been broken in many places. She broke her clavicle when she landed on her hand and arm, which stiffened to absorb the impact. She also needed surgery to repair her leg with a metal plate. She was in the hospital for close to three months after the surgery. In addition to other broken bones, she suffered severe bruising and was in a great deal of pain. She cried out in agony whenever she was moved. She had to wear a half body cast until her second surgery the following July. The incessant itching that visited her under the cast drove her crazy.

Although she missed out on much of her senior year at high school, she held-court with many of her friends who ended up hanging out at the hospital with her, smuggling in burgers and fries. Her friends continued to support her through the painful period of healing. In fact, her drama instructor allowed her to play Dorothy in a leg cast by altering the production for her. She later started college in a full leg cast and crutches. This was not exactly the impression she wanted to make at the freshman college mixer.

Having never broken a bone, I can only imagine her ordeal. My body cringes and shudders at the images. Sharyn recently discovered pictures of herself in the hospital with her swollen face, bruises and full cast. She broke into tears seeing them. Facing traffic while on foot continues to be difficult for her. To this day, we cannot cross a street without her stiffening and clutching my hand, while I protectively try to pull her to the other side of the street when there is a break in traffic. In short, she has persisting Post Traumatic Stress Disorder for anything resembling the original incident.

As part of her experience, she had a telepathic conversation with God, who appeared to her in the form of pure light. As with others who have had this experience, she knows beyond a shadow of a doubt that it was a spiritual revelation and not just a biochemical light/color show postulated by some scientists as an explanation for such experiences. People who have not personally experienced the miracles of light or spirit so common in NDEs and meditation have such a difficult time believing they exist. Those, on the other hand, who have had these experiences, know how undeniably sacred they are.

While such experiences have never been proved to be products of brain chemistry, they may in fact alter it, as Dr. Daniel Amen has shown in *Making a Good Brain Great*. He reports, "We performed SPECT scans at rest one day and then after meditation the next day. We saw marked decreases in the left parietal lobes (decreasing awareness of time and space) and significant increases in the prefrontal cortex (which showed that meditation helped to tune people in, not out). We also saw increased activity in the right temporal lobe, an area that has been associated with spirituality."

Iona Miller writes in her on-line article, *Fear & Loathing in the Temporal Lobes: Epilepsy and Spirituality*: "Subjective experiences are the basis of mysticism and the religious impulse. The brain is hard-wired for mystical experiences, perhaps as an adaptation to soothe the stress incurred in daily life. Peak experiences, raptures, epiphanies, even illumination are potentially available to everyone. Spontaneous transient electrical chaos in the temporal lobes is perfectly normal, making the God experience an artifact of healthy function...The God experience is a process in which one learns to embody spiritual being, infusing life with meaning. The soul soars, freed from the prison of ego, mind and body. It brings in its wake oceanic expansion, suspension of time, space and ego, sudden insight, childlike wonder, exaltation, gnosis, fusion."

There may be correlations between brain chemistry and spiritual experiences, but the fact is that there are aspects of the NDEs that can't be explained by chemistry alone. I will discuss these later in the book.

My wife's experience germinated the idea for this book. However, it was not her near death experience alone that intrigued me. I was fascinated by the amazing similarities it had to my own and others' experiences generated by deliberately focused spiritual practices such as chanting, meditation, and prayer. Of course these expanded experiences of the light of consciousness can also spontaneously visit us as we go about our daily "waking" lives, sometimes stimulated by the beauty of nature, the love of another or some inner thought, feeling or revelation. I was enthralled as Sharyn explained her near death journey to me, not only for the great mystery it holds, but because I knew as she talked, that I had been drawn there, too, without dying.

Whether these experiences occur during near death situations, are spontaneous or are the result of self-directed meditation practices, people are passionate when they speak about experiencing the "Other Side", the "Light of Consciousness", the "Realm of Spirit" or "Heaven". I include myself in this group. The stunning and transforming effects of these experiences signal that something profound has happened. The effects often stay with the person or recur throughout their lives. Some who lived life as a difficult, angry struggle before their experiences report becoming more sensitive and caring people afterwards. Some who were not even believers become not only believers, but in their words, "knowers". Carl Jung was once asked if he believed in God and he answered that he <u>knew</u> God. Others who were depressed or apathetic developed a zest for life. Many become telepathic or clairvoyant. One man's story that Kenneth Ring documents in *Lessons From the Light*, indicates he had such a profound experience of rising upward and being enveloped by a luminous being that he transformed from an atheist to an ordained minister. His book documents many other spectacular transformations.

Both in an NDE and in meditation, the figure/ground relationship of body-mind to spirit is suddenly and dramatically reversed: "reality" (our world-body-mind reality) is experienced as unreal illusory form and the former "non-reality" (spirit) becomes overwhelmingly real. We speak of awakening to a new reality, however, the evidence is that it may be our lack of awareness of the field of ultimate reality (spirit), which is the problem. The reports of those who have had an NDE and the reports of those practicing deep forms of meditation suggest that we are extremely close to spirit at all times.

Sharyn's Near Death Experience

SHARYN'S NDE WAS BEYOND any waking or sleep experience she had ever had before and it contained most of the elements of reported NDEs. She was drawn out of her body toward a light. She experienced an enormous and expanded feeling of well-being. She was in a total state of conscious "knowing" that she was pure spirit in a world woven of spirit. She telepathically heard "without ears" the voice of a higher power directing her to return because it was not yet her time to cross over. She also experienced the true meaning of unconditional, all-pervasive love.

She remembers feeling nothing at impact when she was hit by the car. What she remembers next is being in a "time warp". She knew, not thought, that she was dead. There was no sadness about it; it was just a fact. She remembers separating from her body, leaving it and the accident behind. She felt things speed up as she traveled away from her body, through a dusk-colored space that led to her right to a space of light. She began to feel extremely calm and that "...there was all the time in the world." Everything was incredibly peaceful and joyous. She was in a deep state of bliss. Her exact description to me of what she experienced is as follows:

"Oh! This is that state that people try all their lives to achieve. This is the moment of experience they want to touch, that moment of absolute peace and absolute joy. And I felt that this is 'it' — true happiness . I had this really deep knowing and I knew that it was a wise knowing — I knew it as the truth. I recognized this state — it was familiar and yet a joyful new discovery. I was absolutely delighted to finally be in this state and let myself experience the joy a hundred percent. I remember somersaulting in the bliss and tumbling in it and feeling how good it felt to finally be back in that state. It was like being there again and I had been there before. It wasn't about doing something to make me happy and it wasn't about achieving something to be happy, but it was about experiencing a state with no barriers, no boundaries and no limitations. I knew that this was what people worked all their lives for, whether they expected to experience it through their career, friendships, family or whatever. I had this incredible knowing that 'oh yes', this is

what people try to achieve and now I'm in 'it'. I felt so glad to return here. I was kind of giggly about it; it felt so good and so free. There were no regrets about leaving behind all that was so important to my 16 year old self, and I was the kind of girl who hated to go away for even a weekend with my parents for fear I would miss some exciting part of high-school life."

I asked a question about form. She responded saying, 'it' was absolutely formless and she was formless. There were no boundaries. She said "It was endless, infinite space — empty while being completely full. There were no boundaries and I was not in a form; I was not in a body. I was, if I had to call it anything, a spirit without boundaries that was part of all that was surrounding me. I know — I would say think, but it wasn't 'thinking', it was 'knowing' — I was part of this wonderful, wonderful bliss. "

I asked a question about who knew; who was 'the knower'? She responded, "I was the knower - and I was the known. It was that part of me that is always there, but there wasn't the physicality of me. Even though I was formless, I had an integrity of being myself with only the simplicity and purity of knowing the truth."

I asked the question "where were your boundaries?" She responded, "I have no idea. There weren't any boundaries. I didn't feel any boundaries. Any kind of definition I try to put on it, any kind of description I try to make of it, as soon as I get the description formulated, it is automatically limited because it is not that, it is more than that. So the definition I would give is like being up in the dark blueness of the sky and being able to look out into all infinity and not being able to see the end of anything and just being part of all of it but not feeling any loneliness at all. There was no loneliness. I was just being a part of it. It was just like being in a dark blue, yet clear sparkling pure sky — and, yet, that is not 'it' because that description is too finite, but that is as close as I can come."

I asked a different question about boundaries. She answered, "There was a 'me'ness that was part of the 'sky'ness, and this 'me'ness was this knowing, this crystal clear knowing. It wasn't like going through a process of figuring something out, or thinking about something or contemplating an idea, it was just an immediate knowing. It was knowing/recognizing this peace and joy and recognizing that this was the peace and joy that everybody on earth struggled for because they had a trace memory of the feeling. There were a lot of different ways that people struggled for it, yet there was a sense of disappointment in the process of attempting to attain it because nothing could ever measure up to the supreme feeling of that bliss."

She continued:

"I have to say that what is significant about my experience is that I was 16 years old, I was not philosophical, I had not read any metaphysical material, I was not aware of searching for anything and I was not particularly interested in anything metaphysical or spiritual in nature. Remember this was the 1950s! I was attached to my peer group, my boyfriend, my social life, my active school life and the daily dramas of my friends . I wanted to be connected to what my friends were doing —what the current gossip was, who was on the other end of the phone — certainly not what was happening in another realm of existence!! But in this special place I had entered, all of these feelings and experiences were absolutely unimportant and it was fine to be away from them all because I had entered this space and felt a deep longing of mine satisfied that I didn't even know had existed."

All of what she described occurred in an instant; it was an instant where there was plenty of time, and yet an instant where almost no time had passed. Being and moving were happening at the same time. She was being accelerated in this time warp so there was a feeling of traveling. She was traveling at great speed, leaving the scene of what happened and shooting upward through space. However, she felt there was an eternity in each second of experience. She was very focused. The right side held more light and she was being drawn magnetically deeper into that brighter light.

At this point in her narration to me, she began to get emotional about recounting the experience and began to cry. She said that what is really amazing about the experience is that even though she had the experience when she was 16 years old and it was now many decades later, the experience was as real, as profound, and as meaningful as when she was 16. It was more profound than any event that has happened at any other time in her life. It is clear that it is as if it happened just a moment ago.

She felt she was being drawn toward the light at rapid speed. As she got closer to it, the exquisiteness of the light increased as did her desire to be there. She experienced it as the deepest of loves. She felt total and complete support. This was where she really wanted to be. It was extremely familiar. She describes it as coming home to some place she had been before. She wanted to completely merge with it, and felt she could.

At the last moment, she was told she couldn't stay and would have to go back. Heaven was denied. Paradise was lost. She felt intense disappointment, yet she was being denied with such great love and compassion that she completely accepted the wisdom of the message. She doesn't understand why she was so accepting, but she knew with certainty that going back was the right thing to do.

Sharyn remembers being drawn back to her body, hovering over it, and eventually entering back into it. She remembers everything that was being done to her body by the ambulance attendants below. She saw things from above that couldn't possibly be seen from the vantage point of her body that was laying on the street. As a matter of fact, the report she gave the police confused them so they kept telling her she couldn't have seen the details that she said she did from the tarmac so many feet in front of the car! What was true was that she had two views of the accident and the facts of both turned out to be accurate.

She had the desire to stay forever in the heavenly state she had just experienced. Unlike Dorothy who felt Oz was a strange place and wanted to return home to Kansas, Sharyn felt that the heavenly realm she had entered was her true home. In spite of this, she was told telepathically that it wasn't yet her time and she was drawn back into her body, where she reconnected to the pain of the impact with the car and the road. She relates a strange experience of feeling that her soul didn't instantly fit in her body, as though she was putting on a Halloween mask, discovering that the eye holes were not lined up with her own eyes (the soul's "eyes" in this case).

Following that altered state of the NDE, she was left with the uncanny gift of periodically knowing the future and telepathically receiving information, both of which are a mixed blessing. It is no accident she became a psychotherapist, and a spiritually intuitive one at that.

As intense as this experience was for Sharyn, as is apparent from her own description of it, it is not atypical of NDE's reported by other people. In fact, as people in the personal and spiritual growth field, Sharyn and I both were enthralled with Carl Jung's NDE that he wrote about in his autobiography. He was arguably one of the deepest thinkers and most influential spiritual psychologists in the history of psychology, and had an amazing experience in the hospital during recovery from a heart attack around 17 years before his actual death. Jung ostensibly died and left his body and could view the earth at an estimated thousand miles below him. He too, during this experience, was told to return because it wasn't his time to die.

In *Memories, Dreams and Reflections* he reports becoming aware of floating through space toward a huge stone structure that was a temple, where sat a Hindu. He knew he would be debriefed by beings on the other side about his earthly experiences. As he moved into the structure, a strange and unexpected thing occurred; his soul was intercepted by the attending doctor's soul. An exchange was made telepathically, whereby Jung could return to his much needed work on earth.

Jung described other direct spiritual experiences he had during his convalescence. He saw many of the archetypes about which he wrote come to life as holograms within his room and dance before him in a blue light, surrendering unto him their mysteries. His nurse appeared as if in a blue glow as well.

As might be expected, when Jung awakened and realized he had not died and the doctor had offered an exchange of sorts, he was concerned about the doctor. In the following days of his convalescence, he repeatedly inquired into the doctor's health. Two weeks later, Jung learned his doctor had in fact fallen into a fever and died, while Jung himself recovered. A kind of exchange did seem to have been made.

Sharyn related to me that the communication to her freed soul to return to the earth plane was from a formless God. This was an experience for her of 'knowing' a message from the light. She recognized the higher intelligence in that white light and was informed that this was not her time and that there was a purpose in her life yet to be fulfilled, so she had to return. Because it was a knowing of higher truth, it was easy for Sharyn to accept and follow. She often says about death, "I know two things for certain about death. One is that there is a right time and that time is not solely determined by our own desire. The other thing I know is that there is a purpose to each of our lives and my purpose was yet to be actualized."

She was finally transported to the hospital where she was cacooned in a body cast that was to be her home for some months to follow. Something she feels was a huge help in her eventual recovery from both the accident and from the NDE was that her doctor had had another patient who shared the same kind of story with him and as he had done before with them, he listened openly to her about her experience.

Some readers may not think they have had experiences of other states of consciousness like those in Sharyn's and others NDEs. I want to remind those readers that there are examples of spirit breaking through to us every day, such as when we experience synchronicities that take our breath away or when we are enraptured by the beauty in nature. However, those who insist they have not had a spiritually transforming experience might just need to see one of their everyday experiences (actually, an every night experience) in a different light. They may have forgotten the very magical and rejuvenating nature of a nightly practice common to all.

Waking up to the Magic of Life

I AM ONE OF those who learn by teaching. I have had the good fortune to teach and facilitate meditation since the early 1970's. One of my methods to introduce new students to the alternative realities available to us through meditation is to tell them a story about an alien race that performs unique nightly rituals, using strange powers with even stranger results. These alien group members are very human in appearance. However, they have mysterious powers of rejuvenation. They also have unusual rituals by which they call on these powers. When their planet, in its daily revolution, turns its back to the sun in their solar system and darkness begins to fall, they enter darkened chambers. These storage chambers have been furnished with padded platforms where these creatures store themselves, like a log on a hearth, after their sun disappears from sight.

These creatures have the proclivity for massive shifts in consciousness. At night, they completely abandon their waking state and enter a trance state wherein they travel to subtle inner states of unconscious bliss. Were an observer to walk into one of their storage chambers within an hour of being darkened, these beings might not even notice because they have abandoned waking consciousness so completely. Such is the depth and power of the trance state into which they enter.

The subtle recharging these beings experience in their trance state comes from some deep state of bliss or ecstasy in which they languish all night. The utter blissfulness of this transforming state is apparent when they are signaled to arise from the padded platform by pre-programmed signal tones at the time their side of the planet once again welcomes their sun. Refusing to leave the blissful state of peace in which they have absorbed themselves, many are known to literally burrow in and hug the padding on the platform. Even the pungent smell of a dark energizing herb that is brewed just for the purpose of bringing them out of their trance state fails to break some of them free from the rapture they feel. The young ones have to be drawn out of their trance many times and more and more abruptly because they have not yet learned to "break-bliss" for break-fast.

The nightly rejuvenation of this alien species by this ritual is more or less complete, depending upon how well they abandon their sometimes-cluttered conscious state. Most have been sufficiently recharged by some all-pervasive source to which they surrender, so that they have the energy to resume another day's functioning on their demanding planet. Some are left with symbolic images of guidance from the intelligence of this state to which they retreat. The images are encoded in the symbol-language of the higher intelligence itself. The symbols represent undeveloped aspects of themselves as well as emerging powers and abilities that can be used to overcome weaknesses. These images can act like printouts of a self-diagnosis system similar to some of the ones found in our own computer systems. When interpreted, the images offer guidance for the aliens' focus in their lives. The images also bring great energy pertinent to the symbol they represent that boosts the aliens' systems in needed ways.

If they are ill, at least in the case of more moderate conditions, they awaken at each revolution of the planet not only more refreshed, but also more and more healed. They are so habitualized to this ritual, however, that they have long since forgotten to honor and feel gratitude for the force so crucial to their healing, guidance and replenishment. They have lost their awe of their own sacred daily life and its rituals. They think, "I feel good today after a good night's sleep," instead of thinking "As divine spirit I infused and rejuvenated myself last night and I am steeped in my higher radiance." Such is the power of their and our minds to devalue the experience of spirit and deaden it with language.

This is not true of many of those who have had NDEs, nor, for that matter, for those of us who have dived deeply enough into spiritual practices. Awakening to our living essence actually brings a refreshed and renewed appreciation of the fountain of love, joy and wisdom behind the scenes of our everyday lives. Each moment is precious, even if we miss a few due to our chronic tendency to stay unconscious and unaware. I think those who say they have not had a spiritually transforming experience might want to reevaluate that based upon their nightly meditation we call 'sleep'.

Sharyn's NDE in Comparison

GIVEN THE NIGHTLY EXPERIENCE with altered states of consciousness and the raptures we can feel in nature as we gaze at meadows, forests, lakes, seas and sunsets, perhaps we can open our minds and hearts to the experiences NDErs have during the period they are dead or in coma. In his book, *Transformed By The Light*, Melvin Morse (and P. Perry) lists the different elements of the NDE's that he, Raymond Moody and others have found their subjects to have experienced. Sharyn's, experience contains most of the elements he mentions.

A Sense of Being Dead - Sharyn knew she was going to be hit and probably die. She felt herself leave her body behind and knew she was dead. However, the knowing of being dead was not horrific or frightening nor was her regret about leaving a life she was immersed in. Instead she embraced it, thinking, "Oh, this is that state that people try all their lives to achieve." What was happening to her body was inconsequential because of the joy and bliss of the beyond that dominated her experience.

Peace and Painlessness - Her whole being knew that, "This is the moment we all want to touch into, that moment of absolute peace and absolute joy." Sharyn knew no pain and was in absolute peace. She would not experience pain until she consciously re-entered her broken body.

Out-of-Body Experience - Sharyn said about the state of light, "It was absolutely formless and the only way I could describe being in this space was that there were no boundaries. I was not in a body. I was, if I had to call it anything, a spirit that was part of what is. I was melting with this wonderful, wonderful bliss. She saw the ambulance attendants working over her body as she re-entered it. She was being drawn back into form; a bruised and broken body form.

Tunnel Experience - Many, but not all NDErs report moving through a tunnel towards the light. The tunnel aspect was not present for Sharyn. She was one of those who experienced being drawn at great speed more directly toward a glowing expanse. The space she was immediately in had no boundaries itself. She was moving through the glowing, joyous space at some speed, but at the same time felt like there was, "...all of the time in the world."

People of Light - Sharyn was speeding toward a merging with a brilliant, infinite being of light, but no other beings of light greeted her as a welcoming committee as some of the NDErs experience.

Being of Light - Sharyn remembers that she could not completely merge with the light. The vastness seemed to expand as she traveled into it. She heard it speak and spoke back, but the light, in her words, "...heard without ears and spoke without a voice." She once again cried tears of loving remembrance as she recounted this part of her story.

Life Review - Sharyn's journey to the light after leaving her body was so brief that when she returned, her body still lay on the paved street where she was struck by the car. She does not remember going through a life review as such.

Reluctance to Return - In the split second Sharyn was told she had to go back, she begged and pleaded not to have to return. She wanted to merge with the light. She had returned 'home' only to be told that she must go back. She says that her desire to stay was not related to anything about her life on earth that she particularly wanted to avoid. It was just that all of her earthly life paled in significance in relation to the splendor of the light. The desire to merge in the light caused her to beg and plead. Only with great reluctance did she return after feeling the benevolence of that intelligent field of light and accepting the absolute wisdom of its command. She become aware of the painful condition of her body only after returning.

Personality Transformation - Sharyn says that she was never the same after her experience. She was no longer afraid of death. She knew that we were all a part of something greater. She knew what love and joy awaits us all when we cross over. She knew that she was loved in a way that earthly parents can never duplicate.

When asked by me about the tears she cried, she said, "I don't know. I guess it was just the incredible, incredible love I felt in that presence. Words can't describe it and always reduce it when I try to talk about it. This is the most frustrating part of it for me. It just touches something deep in my soul. It is deeply moving. My head is trying to make sense of something that is an unfathomable experience. It is awesome to think that that kind of love exists and that that kind of order exists. It was being in that kind of splendor that is beyond words."

She again and again repeated how inadequate words are to describe the magnificence of the experience. Only once more in her life did she remember experiencing something similar. It happened when she was in the living presence of a powerful spiritual master to whom I introduced her, but this subject is for a subsequent book.

Sharyn already had a zest for life, but this zest grew nonetheless. She became a marriage and family therapist and has been a spiritual guide for many clients who thought they were coming to see her only for psychotherapy. At times, since her NDE, she has known the future before it happens, even in the simple act of knowing a client will call her in the next 30 seconds, though one could say it was a telepathic knowing that a client is calling. Her whole life has taken a more spiritual direction since then. Each time she thinks about the experience, it is nearly as fresh as the day it happened.

Recently, she was sharing her experience with people on an European tour we joined and Sharyn choked up and shed tears when she shared the glory of the light she encountered. In her NDE, she learned the secret of life. She has since lived her life accordingly, as so many of Morse's subjects report having happened to them. Many other people over the years have reported their NDEs and in the next chapter I want to present some of their experiences with the light. They serve as beacons for all spiritual seekers of what we can have as a daily reality. We only have to seek it, awaken to it, and learn to incorporate it into our ongoing flow of life.

The Glory of the Light

MY AIM IN THIS chapter is to steep the reader in the wonder of NDErs experiences in the hope that this will inspire seekers to discover or rediscover, through introspection, reflection, contemplation and other spiritual practices, their own experience of "The Light" (because this entire book is an ode to "The Light", which I am using as a designation of "The Light of Consciousness", or "God" throughout the book, I will not be using quotation marks around The Light from here on out). Immense hope is available in these experiences that cannot fail to inspire. Perhaps some of the most inspiring encounters with The Light are those of children who have yet to be shaped and formed into any particular religious belief beyond being told that there is a God and that relatives who have died have "gone to heaven".

In *Closer to the Light,* by Melvin Morse, M.D. (with Paul Perry) a four year old girl later in her life reports of her childhood NDE, "I noticed the dim light growing slowly brighter. The source of light was not in the basement (where she fell), but far behind and slightly above me. I looked over my shoulder into the most beautiful light imaginable. It seemed to be at the end of a long tunnel which was gradually getting brighter and brighter as more and more of the Light entered it. It was yellow-white and brilliant, but not painful to look at even directly. As I turned to face the light with my full 'body' I felt happier than I ever had before or have since."

In the same book is a statement by a 14 year old boy written several years later. He writes, "I knew I was either dead or going to die. But then something happened. It was so immense, so powerful, that I gave up on my life to see what it was. I wanted to venture into this experience which started as a drifting into what I could only describe as a long, rectangular tunnel of light. But it wasn't just light, it was a protective passage of energy with an intense brightness at the end which I wanted to look into, to touch. …As I reached the source of the light, I could see in. I cannot begin to describe in human terms the feelings I had over what I saw. It was a giant infinite world of calm, and love, and energy, and beauty. It was as though human life was unimportant compared to this. And yet it urged the importance of life at the same time it solicited death as a means to a different and better life. It was all being, all beauty, all meaning for all existence. It was all the energy of the universe forever in one place. As I reached my right hand into it, feelings of exhilarating anticipation overwhelmed me. I did not need my body anymore. I wanted to leave it behind, if I haven't already, and go to my God in this new world." This is such a peak experience that most people might not relate to it, not having had one like it. However, to know this exists beckons us to find a pathway to it.

I was delighted to see that Morse and Perry, in their above book, included Paramahamsa Yogananda's childhood experience of the light. Though Yogananda did not experience clinical death, nonetheless he was very ill with Asiatic Cholera, which is often a fatal disease. After praying in front of the picture of his parents' Yoga Master, he reports, "There was a blinding light, enveloping my body and the entire room. I was well." The light, to which he refers as a 'luminous blaze' also healed him from the Cholera he was suffering with at the time.

One last childhood experience I want to relate is presented in Dr. Cherie Sutherland's Book entitled *Within the Light*. Much later in her life, a woman remembers the near death experience she had when she was 15. She writes, "Then I remember being in the light, just suddenly being totally engulfed by the light. I'm saying 'engulfed,' but it was very nice. I could perhaps say, 'subsumed'–I'm trying to find positive words and use them in the right sort of way. And suddenly I have the feeling that everything was okay, everything was perfectly alright. That was the feeling I remember most. I have the sense that no other feeling in the world was worth that feeling. I can say it is the most beautiful thing I've felt in my life, but in saying that, it's just words.

It's so difficult to describe. I feel that my whole being, my soul energy, my very essence, was touched upon in that state. It seemed to bring about an opening of my psyche and understanding of the world. And that feeling has stayed with me, it doesn't go away. Sometimes suddenly I flow back into it, it gives me so much energy that I feel I have the perseverance to go through anything, at anytime. And now, especially when I meditate, I have the feeling of total communion, a oneness with every piece of energy in the universe, whether it be negative or positive. It almost gave me a sort of amoral attitude to life. I now have the feeling that there isn't any separate good or evil, but there is a combination of opposites, and that everything is necessary."

The words used to describe the light in these childhood experiences are amazing. There were always superlatives followed by words like 'beautiful light', 'happiest', 'infinite world of calm and love and energy and beauty', 'all being, all beauty, all meaning for all existence', 'all the energy of the universe forever in one place', 'exhilarating anticipation', 'blinding light', 'luminous blaze', 'everything okay', 'most beautiful thing', 'my very essence', and 'a feeling of total communion, a oneness with every piece of energy in the universe'.

There is obviously a theme here. The light seemed to transport these children to an entire energy world of light with positive feelings of peace, bliss, aesthetic pleasure and unconditional love that went far beyond their ordinary life experience. Who among us would not want to visit that state, or, like some of these children desired, would not want to stay in this wonderful transcendent world of light. Some of these were young children who were less religiously doctrinated than most of us adults and yet their descriptions sound sacred. Some of them reported being given deep understanding of the essence of the universe and their soul nature. What wonderful images for us to aspire to in our spiritual development.

Many of the adult experiences mirror the child NDEs though adult NDEs can present clearer goals for those needing a meditative focus; they offer details of a true process of expanding into the light. Anita Mooujani, framing these NDEs as maps of the process of change, not only for us, but for the world, says in her book *Dying to be Me*:

"Realizing that the Light, the Magnificent, is Universal energy within us and is us, changes us as individuals because we're open and ready. In this way, a slower, deeper shift can take place in the world."

Anita's own NDE is amazing. She writes, in *Dying to be Me,* "Love, joy, ecstasy, and awe poured into me, through me, and engulfed me. I was swallowed up and enveloped in more love than I ever knew existed. I felt more free and alive than I ever had."

Later in her book, she continues, "I was transformed in unimaginable clarity as I realized that this expanded, magnificent essence was really me. It was the truth of my being. The understanding was so clear: I was looking into a new paradigm of self, becoming the crystalline light of my own awareness."

I love the last phrase "… becoming the crystalline light of my own awareness." This light is described by others as crystalline as well; like the purest of light that would emanate from a diamond. One of the NDE participants mentioned in Kenneth Ring's studies in *Heading Towards Omega*, shares:

"At first I became aware of beautiful colors which were all the colors of the rainbow. They were magnified in crystallized light and beamed with a brilliance in every direction. It was as if all this light was coming at me through a prism made by a most beautiful and purified diamond, and yet at the same time it was as if I were in its center. I was in a heavenly pasture with flowers. It was another place, another time, and perhaps it was even another universe. But it was definitely another consciousness–vibrant and more alive then the one I had known in my earthly life. My ears were filled with the music so beautiful no composer could never duplicate it. It too was not of this world. It was soothing, gentle, and warm and seemed to come from a source deep within me."

And later in his account of his NDE, he says:

"This magnificent light seemed to be pouring through a brilliant crystal. It seemed to radiate from the very center of the consciousness I was in and to shine out in every direction to the infinite expanses of the universe. I became aware that it was part of all living things and that at the same time all living things were a part of it. I knew it was omnipotent, that it represented infinite divine love. It was as if my heart wanted to leap out of my body towards it. It was almost as though I had met my maker. Even though the light seemed thousands and thousands of times stronger than the brightest sunlight, it did not bother my eyes. My only desire was to have more and more of it and to bathe in it forever."

This idea of bathing in the light represents a partial merging with it, feeling its love, joy and support for all things in the universe. Of course, there is never a final merging for those with NDEs, just as there can not be a final merging for the meditator, nor even a meditation master while embodied. In the latter case, devotees celebrate the date their master left his or her body and completely merged with the divine (though the master is considered to have merged prior to that into some nearly final state of divinity).

NDErs always come back to their bodies, or we would classify them as dead and gone. Many tell tales of choosing to come back and others tell tales of being told to come back by some other higher authority of light. So, as we consider their accounts, we can only imagine how much more complete their experience might be if they merged completely with the divine light. Some of the NDEs seem to have allowed something close to merging, which is shared as an ecstatic experience for the beholder.

One such man mentioned in Kenneth Ring's book, *Heading Towards Omega*, had an experience while under water as he nearly drowned. He shares with us:

"You then realize that you are coming to the end of this tunnel and that this light is not just a brilliance from what ever is at the end of the tunnel–it's an extremely brilliant light. It's pure white. It's just so brilliant...."

And then again later, "The next sensation is this wonderful, wonderful feeling of this light.... It's almost like a person. It is not a person, but it is a being of some kind. It is a mass of energy. It doesn't have a character like you would describe another person, but it has a character in that it is more than just a light, it is so bright but it doesn't hurt your eyes, but it's brighter than anything you've ever encountered in your whole life. At that point, I had no consciousness anymore of having a body it was just pure consciousness. And this enormously bright light seemed almost to cradle me. I just seem to exist in it and be part of it and being nurtured by it and the feeling just became more and more and more ecstatic and glorious and perfect. And everything about it was - if you took the 1000 best things that ever happened to you in your life and multiplied by 1 million maybe you could get close to this feeling, I don't know. But you are just engulfed by it..."

Kenneth Ring sums up some of his participants descriptions of their NDEs as indicating some degree of merging with the light. In *Heading Towards Omega*, he summarizes their experiences:

"The implication is that qualities of the light somehow infuse themselves into the core of the experiencer's being so as to lead to a complete union with the light. And apparently the sense in which medieval theologian and mystic Meister Eckhart spoke of man becoming God, NDErs may experience this merging of their own individuality with the divine. In any event, the testimony from more than one core NDEr indicates that there is a direct transmission of the light's energy into themselves and that what is absorbed in that encounter with the light in that moment outside of time remains with them when they return to the world of time..."

There are so many accounts of experiences of the light in peoples' STEs and NDEs that It would take a book just to list them. Here, I wanted only to pick a few that speak to the "glory of the light". The adult experiences speak of the light in similar, but sometimes different ways that are equally inspiring as the childhood experiences. The adults were obviously more verbal.

The keywords and phrases for adult NDErs included, but were not limited to, 'awe', 'ecstacy', 'enveloped in more love than I knew existed', 'more free and alive', 'the magnificent essence was really me' and 'crystalline light of my own awareness'. Others include 'lights of the rainbow… magnified in crystallize light and beamed with a brilliance in every direction'. And again, 'the light…was part of all living things and…all living things were part of it'. Finally, they included 'most magnificent, just gorgeous, beautiful, bright, white or blue-white light', and 'this enormously bright light seemed almost to cradle me'.

It is hard for us to imagine being cradled in such love even once, let alone constantly. Yet the challenge for us in life seems to be to be established in this love as a daily state of being. I hope by the end of the book I have left enough of a trail of breadcrumbs, which are not all eaten by the birds (of doubt) that can lead the reader to some of these experiences themselves. But first, what is it about these experiences that convinces us they are sacred, rather than biochemical in nature?

These experiences are far beyond what life in the world provides to us and are almost too blissful to describe in words. Something truly divine has shown itself to these NDErs and as we will see, it also reveals itself to people who have not had an NDE, perhaps particularly those who pursue their own spiritual path and are awakened to The Light.

The Transforming Power of the Light

SOMEONE WHO HAS EXPERIENCED the Light of Consciousness has been shown an aspect of transcendent life, usually, though not always, full of the joy of freedom, the contentment of unconditional love and the ecstasy of bliss. They know what lies ahead for them after death and they bring back with them a greater appreciation for their everyday lives. Unlike those who might forget the power and magic of our being, those who have a spiritually transforming experience most often claim they are more awake to life's mysteries.

One might be tempted to consider a solely physiological explanation for the experience of divine light in near death experiences (NDEs) and spiritual practices, were it not for some aspects of these experiences that demonstrate a consciousness or universal mind is an integral part of them. It has been shown that particular biochemical reactions and brain activities accompany deep meditation. However, assuming the experiences of divine light are experiences of the creative aspect of the universe, one might expect that the brain, itself a product of divine creation, would in fact have modalities to allow spirit to manifest and be experienced by each one of us.

Paramahamsa Yogananda, whose experience of the light as a boy was shared above, is one of the spiritual masters responsible for yoga meditation being imported to America from India. He taught that the body's genetics were designed by the divine to dispense a person's karmas; their "lot in life" that they earned from past life times. Science can't test the truth of this at the present time. However, if experiences of divine light are valid, why wouldn't the physical vehicle be designed for habitation by the soul, including physical characteristics that allow the higher states to manifest through the body as higher states of light consciousness and, as Yogananda suggested, karmas?

Lasting Transformations

Several aspects of these experiences do not fit the scientific suggestion that NDEs are merely biochemical or neurological effects. A major problem for which the scientist must account, is that people report that they are so deeply touched by their encounters with what they describe as unimaginable love and peace that their lives are literally transformed by the power of it. To use a lasting fictional classic as a metaphor, consider Dickens' Scrooge. His encounters with beings from the other side of the veil completely transformed his life. People who experience NDEs have often been given an experience, that makes even the most cynical of them offer their lives to divine service.

Dr. PMH Atwater lists a number of transformations she sees in her research that are generally experienced by NDErs. I discuss them more fully below. Dr. Melvin Morse was drawn to this aspect of the NDE and wrote about it in his second book, *Transformed by the Light*. He found overwhelming evidence of this transformation in the lives of the NDErs he studied. Kenneth Ring also points to these transformations in one of his later books, *Lessons from the Light*. This fact of life transformation alone speaks against the merely biochemical hypotheses for NDEs or meditation experiences and suggests that there in fact is a higher state of consciousness, a loving intelligence, that infuses the person having the experience with lasting qualities such as love and compassion that motivate a person to grow and change in a positive direction. The encounter with The Light was permanently uplifting for the recipients.

Perceptions Outside the Ocular Range

Kenneth Ring, in the above referenced book, validates another challenge for the physical model of NDE experiences. He demonstrates evidence of a consciousness that permeates NDEs that allows unusual perceptions not available to the NDEr in their waking life. In one such case, one of his subjects, while reportedly out of body, saw a red shoe on a window ledge of a different floor of the hospital than she was in, which was not visible to her from her room.

Some higher perception is involved, not just biochemicals. Atwater, in a recent talk that I attended, mentioned a study of a number of people that died briefly together and then were separated in a hospital and revived, all recounting the same NDE experience, including interactions with each other during their joint OBEs, even though they had not discussed their experiences with each other due to the separation to be transported to the hospital. The biochemical explanation falls short for these kinds of experiences.

That is not to rule out that the higher states manifest through the body via biochemical changes that allow the body to experience the higher states involved. For example, Winkelman, in his work *Shamans, Priests and Witches: A Cross-Cultural Study of Magico-Religious Practioners*, states, "When ritualized shamanic performance is described as 'archetypal', the activity reflects biologically based modes of consciousness, a replacement of the ordinary waking state through discharge patterns that produce inter-hemispheric synchronization and coherence, limbic-cortex integration, and integral discharges that synthesize cognition, affect, and behavior." Anyone who has taken the drugs LSD or Ecstasy can vouch for altered states of consciousness generated by the biochemical changes produced by these and other drugs. However, even in these drug-altered states, there often seems to be access to authentic higher states of consciousness as at least part of the experience; light, bliss, ectacy and divine imagry are common.

Higher Guidance

Another non-biological and more spiritual aspect of NDE's is the actual guidance that comes from them, which one would not expect if they were merely a cellular event. People who have had one of these experiences come away knowing that there is a divine intelligence within the loving light they experience. Their encounter feels extremely intimate because it is a feeling of shared rapture with an all-pervasive, loving, and in some cases, star-tlingly, all-knowing presence, which actually guides them through difficult choices they have to make in the midst of difficult times. An encounter with a presence which is at once pure love and infinite mind, but which is also experienced as disembodied, can understandably be life altering. In my wife's case and many cases discussed by the authors I've mentioned, there was a telepathic communication (for want of a better phrase), or a "knowing", received from the light that imparted the idea that it was not their time to merge with it and that instead they would have to return to their lives on earth.

I was recently meditating at the center I attend and was aware of a per-sonal financial issue that was fairly complicated, involving some inheri-tance monies, some mortgage issues and my relationship with Sharyn. Consciously, I was stumped and locked up tighter than Pandora's box about possible solutions. As I meditated my state brightened and expanded, and without thinking the problem through, the expansion of consciousness brought the gift of an epiphany. The solution, fully articulated, arrived as an entire package, to be unwrapped all at once. On my own, I would never have thought of this brilliant solution. It was delightful and freeing. When I shared it with Sharyn she said "Of course! Why didn't I think of that!" There is no question in my mind that a higher consciousness communicated to me a complicated message in an instant. Some guidance and illumination, innate to the higher states of light I moved into, responded to my dilemma. This has become a major way I evaluate choices in my daily life. It is listening to that often faint voice or having an image appear that holds a solution.

I recall a particular meditation of mine in the early 1990's where I seemed to be lost in a black tunnel. I was also feeling a little lost in my life at that time due to struggles relating to my work, and was crying out silently for direction. The tunnel seemed as dark and confining as were certain isolated areas of my life, and fear was flooding my system. I sat that way for over an hour. As I reached out in prayer and repeated over and over again a mantra that I had been using for years in meditation, an unexpected response occurred. I had experienced the power of mantras before and knew the power of their vibratory induction. As I repeated the prayers and mantras, rather than a hand, face or being of light appearing to reassure me, the walls of the dark tunnel itself moved ever so slightly. The walls themselves displayed a darkly glimmering, slowly brightening chiaroscuro or numinosity, a subtly conscious quality that was unmistakably alive. It was like seeing a dark corner of a cave suddenly move and realizing it was the presence of a bear, a living creature. I realized with surprise and delight that the dark tunnel itself (no creature needed), which completely surrounded me, was itself a darkened form of the light of divine consciousness!

The effect in this experience was similar to my first experience with the books of pictures that, when concentrated on, produce a figure/ground shift. Most of us, at one time or another, have stared at figure/ground pictures; creatively designed pictures of vases or some object that shift to the background as we gaze at them. After focusing on the objects for a period of time, the spaces in between them pop out as figures of some sort, such as a person's head, while the objects (images of vases) originally stared at become the background. If we continue to concentrate on the "new" configuration, it will then flip back to the original scene where images of the vases can once again be seen as foreground.

In my meditation, the foreground (figure) upon which I was concentrating, the dark tunnel, eventually flipped into a background, while what was at first background, the hidden light of consciousness, emerged as figure or foreground. The effect, though, was extremely startling and, of course, more meaningful than the figure/ground shifts in pictures designed to produce that shift. There was, what Carl Jung called, a numinous feeling to the shift, as if the robes of God brushed me as he/she passed by.

As I was mesmerized by this shift in my meditation, the ratio of light to dark changed. As the darkness of the cave walls metamorphosed into light, I found myself gripped by an exquisite state of expanded brilliance. The darkness dissipated. It was like an oppressive fog burning off, as the sun's rays transformed it, to reveal the brilliance of the sun, which was there all of the time. I experienced myself surrounded by a living intelligence (my own higher nature) that had responded directly to my earthly communications.

It was a divine game of hide and seek. The loving and playful message being "Don't be alarmed, I have been hiding here all the time." What was revealed to me by experience and a shared knowing, was that even darkness (and perhaps a dark mood) itself, if penetrated by prayer or examined with sensitivity, would be discovered to be an alive state of being. What a great cosmic joke it was! As human beings, we are so adept at hiding ourselves from ourselves and it is so delightful to find our selves, and especially our true Self.

I want to share one of the poems I wrote in the early 1970's during the time I was directing a crisis service in the San Francisco Bay Area, some years before my tunnel experience in meditation. A volunteer for the service, Dennis Bohn, put together a prose and poetry volume entitled *We Are Not Just Daffodils*. Volunteers and staff alike contributed poetry to this project. This is one of several poems spawned by my meditation awakenings back then that seems to capture this play of figure/ground in spiritual experience:

AWAKENING

The Gossamer wings of light
Play upon the cracks of existence
Until one day, when all is calm,
They glisten
Riding the wind of the night
To bring the dawning of a day so bright

That darkness melts into its source

This early poem of mine came to mind as I was recently reading Dr. Alexander's book after hearing his talk at Sofia University. In his book he says the heavenly beings he saw had trails of light flowing behind them, which reminded me of the phrase in my poem "Gossamer wings of light."

I was delighted and moved by the tunnel experience I had and was profoundly impacted. How could I ever again doubt the omnipresence of that great light, showing up in even the darkest corners of my life? Upon later reflection, it seemed as though this might have been a glimpse of the mystery at the core of a later stage of spiritual development called "The Dark Night of the Soul", wherein even the most devout seekers report that their meditations are full of darkness over a period of time, often after years of regular meditation practice when they expected to have become even more predictably established in light. Apparently, darkness itself can be discovered to be only one of the many living cloaks or costumes of The Light.

Certainly, my wife's NDE experience, and other people's NDEs, has that figure/ground aspect as well, where our ordinary reality flips and what is behind and within it shines forth. The "figure", while we are in our bodies, is so often the body itself. We are so captured by its physicality and many demands for basic attention that it stays consistently "figure" for most of our lives. We work to clothe and feed it. We get close to someone who will stroke it and tend to it. We lather and oil it with perfumed substances. We indulge it with thousands of experiences to satisfy it: "More and better wine", it cries, "Nouvelle Cuisine", it cries, "Peets cappuccino, or maybe Starbucks", it screams, "Burger King", it whispers and "Ben and Jerry's", it demands. We exercise it to keep it in shape. We use it to earn our keep. Our physical lives take up most of our time and attention while we are stationed planet-side.

Along with our body's senses being 'figure' for us, a multitude of thoughts, feelings, attitudes and moods are also prominent as foreground objects in most of our lives. How many waking hours are we tracking, and often struggling, with these fluctuating waves of thoughts and emotions, feeling that our life is shaped more by those we have yet to control, than by those upon which we have more of a grip? Life seems to be full of challenges to our success, our esteem, our performance and our control. Sometimes it seems life is more about putting out fires than burning the path we want through its jungle. Then, when awakened, when the experience of The Light becomes foreground, even for a brief instant, all of that changes and the true purpose of life is revealed to us. Then, we are motivated to seek the light in every aspect of our lives, knowing that it has always been there somewhere as background, and we know with certainty that we need to discover it in more and different areas of our lives. The urge to transform ourselves is now conscious in us.

On an NDE website, http://www.near-death.com/experiences/evidence05.html, Dr. PMH Atwater writes on the subject of post NDE transformaitionsin an article called *People are dramatically changed by NDEs*. She says in that article, "What was once foreign becomes familiar, what was once familiar becomes foreign." I think this might be her way of acknowledging the shift that ocurs revealing that we had life backwards; what seemed most prominent in our perception was "reality" and the rest must be superstition. If lucky, or fated, we then awaken to the reverse; what was backdrop to our lives is the true reality, with our life being more of a play of that background consciousness.

Perhaps not every person experiencing a near death experience or some other spiritually transforming experience will act on a new motivation to grow and change, but if awakened by their experience and if their external lives don't block it, most will show transformation towards increased empathy, love and joy in their lives. Even just a glimpse of the background context within which we live our lives can turn our lives around and provide huge motivation for such positive change. I think of asking a fish what water is. They probably aren't that aware of it as something special because it is always their background element. In the same way, we always move in an infinite field of spirit, but if asked, most of us would not have become that aware of that background medium to our daily lives. The moment we do, our lives are never the same.

Except Ye Turn and Become as Little Children

A LINE IN THE poem I shared in the last chapter reads, "The Gossamer wings of light play upon the cracks of existence…" I wrote this before I was ever exposed to Joseph Chilton Pierce's book, *The Crack in the Cosmic Egg*, where he talks about the same metaphoric crack, or doorway, in the 'Cosmic Egg' that allows the divine light to shine through and illumine us. I first slipped through the crack and experienced the other side in my early childhood, though I did not have an NDE. The experiences I had were both frightening and awe inspiring at the time, and were a total mystery to me. They were not so clearly spiritual experiences as was Sharyn's NDE, but were the precursors for me of later spiritual awakening and knowledge. In that sense they might be better considered STEs.

One night some years ago, Sharyn and I were watching a re-run of the the series *Ghost Whisperer* on TV. She looked over at me during the opening scenes where the Ghost Whisperer is a little girl and realizes she has special powers. Sharyn said, "You are tearing up; this is just the opening of the program, which you have seen before." I was tearing up over the scene where, as a little girl of around eight years of age, the ghost whisperer sees the ghost of the man being buried at a funeral. She is asked by the ghost to tell his wife, who is obviously present, things he never got a chance to say to her while alive. At the little girl's request, he arms her with knowledge of special, intimate moments he and his wife shared so his wife would believe the little girl that he was present at his own funeral. When the little girl walks over and relays his affirmations of love, the deceased's wife begins to cry.

I told Sharyn that I feel tears each time I see this because I relate to the little girl. She senses things others might not be aware of, and has knowledge and perception to which others have dulled their awareness. I saw an example of this sensitivity children can have in a group email of things kids will say. Brittany (age 4) had an ear ache and wanted a baby aspirin. She tried in vain to take the lid off the bottle. Seeing her frustration, her Mom explained it was a child-proof cap and she (mom) would have to open it for her. Eyes wide with wonder, the little girl asked, "How does it know it's me?" For Brittany, the bottle and cap were conscious and aware. The Ghost Whisperer as a child touches my heart because she was able to help an adult using her extra sensitivities. In this case she sees she has done something helpful with them and is acknowledged and thanked by her grandmother.

In my particular case, either no one knew about my sensitivities, or, in the case of my father, I was criticized for any sign of such things. These sensitivities occurred and came to my attention while living in a small house in a small town in the least populated state of the United States. It was between the ages of eight and eleven (similar to the young Ghost Whisperer) when these experiences happened to me. It was that time of childhood when curiosity is the driving force. I began thinking a lot about how things worked. I wanted chemistry sets and books on hypnotism for Christmas. I dissected grasshoppers and other bugs, and studied everything I didn't understand (I actually have never lost that drive). I also sensed underlying feelings and attitudes that my parents were either not aware of or denied that drove them into incessant arguing. I seemed to be more sensitive to the underlying dynamics of their relationship than they were, but they criticized me if I ever suggested these things to them. As it turned out, I was also sensitive to higher states of consciousness, as probably most children are, although I didn't understand it at the time.

I liked to be outside during the summer months, especially in the evening. One such lazy, warm evening the smell of sweet peas that I planted for my mom and the lilacs she loved so much permeated the night air. People were inside their houses in our neighborhood with doors open, the sounds of radios playing, kids laughing, parents dispensing do's and don'ts and aromas of cooking foods wafting across the street. I was glad to be outside in the otherwise still of the night.

The stars in Wyoming seemed extraordinarily bright, at least in my childhood memories. Perhaps we were closer to them at the 5,300-foot elevation Lander enjoyed. Or perhaps the smog-free air created a clearer lens for that perception. I loved the smell and feel of grass, though I remember that the moisture on it at night would seep through my clothes and make me itch. I could smell the freshly mowed clover in the field across from our house and could hear a symphony of crickets. Livestock nearby made their nighttime sounds. These moments took on such a special feeling that I would roll around on the front lawn like a golden retriever rolling around in dog heaven. I was thrilled to be alone in the night, filling my senses with all of the experiences that the freshness of youth allowed me to notice and appreciate.

The main feast, though, was above. The sky was such a mystery. To my curious, awe-filled child's mind, those diamonds of light which were so far away that they were mere pinpoints in a gigantic sphere, were absolutely magical. I would lie on my back and become absorbed in the spectacle above. It was immense. I wanted to stare at it all together, but this was impossible. I would let my stare become diffuse to see it all, but then I would lose detail. Then I would focus on a particular constellation of stars and marvel at their shape and brilliance. I would pick out the big and little dipper. I would wonder how they were so clearly shaped in the dark of the night sky.

Then I would begin to feel the wonder and awe at the immensity of it all. How could my child's mind make sense of something so huge and mysterious? So many questions arose. How far away were the stars? Which ones were the close ones and which ones were far away? How far away were the farthest? If they were the farthest away, what was beyond them? How far did the sky go beyond the farthest of them? Was the curve at the further most reach of the sky a round boundary of the sky marking the end of the sky? If it wasn't the end of the sky, why did it appear round instead of boundary-less. If it was the end of the sky then what existed beyond it? If there was 'nothing' beyond it, what was 'nothing' made of? The sky itself seemed to be made of nothing. But if the sky was made of nothing, then what was the difference between the sky on this side of the end of the universe and the sky on the other side? If this side was sky and 'nothing' was beyond that, then are we are back to what was 'nothing' made of?

If the round far edge of the sky was not a boundary and the sky went on forever, then how far was forever? 'Forever' was hard to grasp. I didn't even know the word 'infinite' at that point. As I contemplated 'forever,' though, a strange thing would begin to happen. It was as if my mind began to expand to fill the void I was calling 'forever'. However, it was an expansion I experienced throughout my body. Some subtle mental radar within me was drawn into an expansion, at great speed, to fill the void, giving me the sensation of winged travel. It was similar to the altered state we experience on a roller-coaster that also expands us beyond our normal experience of walking or riding in a car and leaves us spacey with shakey legs when back on the ground.

As I contemplated the forever nature of space, I entered an ever-expanding state of "space travel" that would continue as long as I stayed focused on the 'forever' of the sky. The experience immobilized me as long as my focus remained. I was in a suspended state of expansion, traveling in all directions at once, experiencing directly the immensity of it all and losing myself in its wonder. I would remain in and out of that state until my mother would call me in for bed.

After my first such experience with the night sky, I was never the same. It was a secret because I had no words by which to communicate it. Who would stay in a conversation with an eight to eleven year old kid long enough to hear about a contemplative thought process which would produce such weird results? Who could I tell? Who would listen? How could I possibly explain it in words? It was so frustrating that I kept it to myself. Only in my adult life would I revisit the experience and understand it in light of adult travel on the spiritual path.

I suspect that many children touch upon this kind of experience, some perhaps diverting their attention at the first moment of discomfort that the experience brings and quickly weighing the experience along side their collective training about such things (don't act so weird, don't talk about such strange things, quit staring like that and so on) and move on to something else. Others, like myself, might follow the strangeness, but not talk about it until much later. As an adult, when I finally was introduced to Joe Pierce and heard him speak several times, he always made me feel better when he spoke about a major study of children and intelligence that showed only one really significant difference from other children in a group of children rated both brilliant and happy: they were allowed more "open-eyed-staring" by their parents than other children! He used to raise the question that maybe they were allowed and encouraged to contemplate or meditate, or at least go within. He made open-eyed staring a positive. Though I may not have indulged in it enough to become both brilliant and happy, I am happy!

Maybe the only difference between some children (who might touch the experience, but move away from it) and myself is that I was so curious about it that this expansion became a guest that I would invite in at other times in my child-life, comfortable or not. I would continue to visit the night sky whenever I would remember to. The results were predictable, though each expansion would leave me feeling a little incomplete. I could never lose myself enough to finish the journey to "forever". I never quite got there. However, the expansion that served as my contemplative space-vehicle began to show up at other times, one of these being my regular nap-time.

I was a very active third grader, and I suspect that my mother could only find peace by occasionally putting me down for a nap. It may have been something I needed to calm me down and allow me to collect my energies, which as you know by now could get scattered all over the universe! But nap-time wasn't something that I thought I needed. I resisted that time like it was death. However, it was a time that became more interesting after my first expansion into space.

After my mother told me that I had to lie there for an hour on the bed, I would eventually close my eyes. I noticed that there appeared to be open space in front of my closed eyes. I would learn to play the same game with that inner space that I learned to play with the night sky. I would first let my gaze become diffuse. I discovered that if I focused in that diffuse way upon the dark inner sky, I could recreate that feeling that it went on and on in front of me. I would begin to expand into that imagined space much as I did the night sky. I learned to call this experience 'buzzing'. As I expanded into that inner space, I would begin to buzz all over, much as an electromagnetic field hums or buzzes as it intensifies. But then an alarming thing would begin to happen. As I expanded and experienced the sensation of falling or traveling in all directions at once, the buzzing would increase, and that would lead to a sense of being immobilized. I felt that I could not voluntarily move my arms or legs.

The more I gave into the experience, the more paralyzed I became. I would play on the edge of fear, one part of me wanting to shout to mom to come rescue me from this strange state, the other side of me wanting to give in even more to this peculiar sensation of 'space travel'. The state of expansion would so captivate me that I was held hostage by its power. I was in its grip and could not, or would not, get free. The buzzing feeling was pleasant, but the expansion, like the speed of a fast car, was both exhilarating and frightening. The paralysis that accompanied it was most frightening of all. As long as I was focused upon the expansion, my entire body was immobilized. This gave the illusion of paralysis. However, I held the effect in place with my fascination in the expansion and my willed absorption in it.

I discovered that if I began to focus instead on my limbs and try to move them, that with repeated efforts, I would eventually find success. A small movement would seem to call my consciousness back to my body and give me the energy for an even larger movement, which would then call even more of my attention and energy, which would allow me to repeat the process. Eventually, some part of my body would become free and then others would soon follow. However, I was stiff after these journeys and needed to move around to get my body back to its usual flexible condition. If only my mom knew what nap-time meant to me! But how on earth could a boy those ages tell anyone about his secret nap time 'space travels?' Neither the words nor the courage was there to allow me to share these strange experiences. And they became more bizarre, not less.

Nights became both exciting and nightmarish. My 'space ship' decided that nighttime was a good time to travel. The experiences at night, though, had a strange quality that nap times never did. Many nights, as I closed my eyes and began to fall asleep, an expansion would begin to occur. However, unlike at nap-time. it had a decidedly visual aspect to it as well. I would open my eyes (or at least think I did) to discover that the walls of my room were expanding into space. I would look at a windowed wall and it would travel away from me at some regular speed. I would shift my gaze to another wall with a door in it and it too would be traveling away from me into space. I would look at the light switch across the room from my bed only to see the wall it was on travel away too. I once again would become more and more immobilized as the space around me expanded.

During the period of time I was writing this last section I happened to be reading Deepak Chopra's novel *The Angel is Near*. The synchronicity of my content and his content leads me to want to share it with you. One of his characters, Michael, witnesses an angel talking to an old woman. The author writes:

*"Michael felt stunned. He had seen too much for that. He felt as if the room were invisibly expanding. It had no walls anymore, but extended beyond his senses, stretching to meet a horizon that would always be just out of reach, even though God was certainly beyond, keeping watch. Afterward, when reality returned to something like its normal state, this feeling would remain with him as a kind of initiation."*as

Chopra used the sensation of expansion to represent "a kind of initiation." Michael's so-called initiatory experiences were very similar to my voyages into the night sky and my nightly expansions into "forever". The physical sensation of the walls expanding with my state was startling and dramatic. I would try as hard as I could to stand up and move to the light switch, but just as when I was napping, I could not move. I would try again and again but felt paralyzed. The expansion had a definite life of its own and once begun would have its way. I wonder now why I was not more frightened than I was. I hated the feeling of paralysis. I would strain against it again and again, but I was never frightened of the expansion that caused it. It seemed a natural progression, logically following from my attempt to relate to the vast expanse of space. It was simultaneously a new adventure and an old friend.

Just as with my nap-time, at night I would eventually be able to move my head a little to sit up. As my head would move, or a foot or an arm would respond, I seemed to begin to draw my energy back to the body level. As this process began, it seemed to reverse the expansion little by little and I would eventually be able to sit and walk towards the light switch. With the light on, the walls would be in place and, though having a stiff body, things would return to normal. Sometimes when I got up to turn on the light, the wall that the light switch was on would continue to expand and as I walked towards it would recede from my reach. I would repeat this over and over in a frustrating attempt to move out of the altered reality the expansion brought with it. I would finally reach the switch, turn it on, only to find myself still in bed with the light off and the walls moving away and expanding; I had walked to the wall as a disembodied soul in an energy body while still having an out of body experience, or OBE.

Only later in adult life did I discover what these experiences were when I began to have them again. After beginning to meditate regularly as an adult, I would fall asleep at night and get into the same state of expansion I experienced as a child. In that state, I would feel the urge to urinate. I would strain to get up and go the bathroom, finally succeed, urinate in the toilet with all of the normal feeling of release, and then realize that I was still in bed and still had to urinate. I came to realize, with my adult mind and storehouse of adult experience, that I was being drawn into an OBE, which seemed real, except for the extreme amount of effort needed to get up.

The body paralysis I experienced while 'out of body' as an adult was the same as the childhood experience and the repeated effort needed to ulti-mately break the spell and return to the body was very similar. With the soul or spirit floating or 'traveling' outside the physical body, there is little left behind to animate the body. Anima is one name for soul because it ani-mates the physical vehicle. With my soul expanding and moving away from body density into finer spiritual states, there was little left 'at home' to move the body when an infinitesimal part of my will attempted to do that.

Other even more dramatic OBEs occurred as an adult, especially after meditating the evening before, which convinced me that the nighttime experiences when I was a child had the same basic structure. That would explain the experience of the walls themselves expanding. It was not a physical event, but an experience in another dimension of reality experienced while out of my body. Some psychic representation of physical reality was showing me my potential to expand, even though the physical world itself remained fixed.

These OBEs didn't always precede an experience with The Light as the OBEs of most NDErs do, but in many respects, they do mimic their OBEs and count as one of the similarities between their NDEs and my meditation-lubricated OBEs I experienced in both childhood and adulthood.

I suppose that some people upon hearing about these experiences might wonder if I was psychotic or otherwise disturbed as a child. I actually was as normal as apple pie (apart from issues most children have who are from somewhat dysfunctional families!). I played hard, had a best friend and ate like a horse. I was adventuresome, being Tarzan one day and Robin Hood the next. I used to make my own bow and arrows out of willow and rose bush suckers. The willow bows were full of spring and sent arrows plenty far for a boy of my age. Rose suckers were straight and stiff with chicken feathers on the end conveniently provided by my friend's parents who had a chicken coop. They would fly straight and true to their mark (yes the thorns and bark were removed). Spent shell casings gathered from my dad's hunting trips would make a good blunt tip for the arrows. These weapons actually felled an occasional rabbit or bird further up from my best friend's property in a grove of Cottonwood trees. They also felled a chicken I deviously aimed at, which did not please my best friend's mother. However, it was served up that night on our dinner plates, floured, spiced and fried.

My parents hunted, fished, hiked, looked for Native American relics and camped almost every other weekend. They always took me along and showed me how to do everything involved. I would run and climb, using my lasso to pull me up the faces of rock formations I would climb (I was Roy Rogers or Gene Autry) to find a perch where I could see the forest and lake below and surprise the bad guys when they came by. I knew how to inflate a rubber raft, put up a tent, cook on a Coleman stove, fish with wobblers, bait and flies, shoot pistols and rifles, and pack and unpack pickup trucks with camping gear. I was given a great appreciation and respect for nature. I was a fairly normal Wyoming child.

My appreciation for the night sky was an easy transition from the appreciation of the forest and lake below from the top of a high ridge of rocks.

It's just that my expansion into the night sky awakened something in me, which I would only later in my adult life understand and appreciate for what it was. Only in adult life would I realize that I wasn't the only child having divinely inspired adventures. I think that when we are children, we are even closer to the expansion and play of spirit, especially before we are taught to label it and divide it into good and bad, acceptable and unacceptable.

The Playfulness Of Pure Spirit

I REMEMBER A STORY told to me by my Jungian Analyst in the 1970's. He was a disciple of Paramahamsa Yogananda, one of the first eastern spiritual masters to bring meditation to the west. The story was about a Christmas celebration which was to be centered around a talk by Paramahamsa Yogananda himself and embodies the child-like playfulness of pure spirit, which, as a playful child, I discovered again and again. As the story goes, the resident monks in Yogananda's Mother Ashram were all concerned about their master's talk taking place at the time it was scheduled and were being rather serious about the logistics of the Christmas program. They were a bit obsessed with doing things right. Their fussiness, though, may not have reflected the spirit of the occasion. And so one of the monks went looking for Yogananda because he was due to speak next as the key speaker of the event. He was nowhere to be found. Nor was his special guest, another revered swami from India, who was going to be part of the presentation that day.

The monk looked here and looked there and was becoming upset that he couldn't find the two focal points of this serious, seasonal event surrounding the celebration of the birth of Christ. He had looked in Yogananda's room, and in every other room of the ashram, and found them all empty. His second visit to Yogananda's room found it empty again. This time, however, he heard a strange sound coming from the balcony outside of the room. It was a "varoom, varoom" and then the sound of gears whining and spinning. He approached the balcony. Again he heard, but from another voice at the opposite end of the balcony, "varoom, varoom" and then the gear and wheel sound coming from that direction. Then he saw the ochre robe of his master.

Paramahamsa was seated on the floor of the balcony. The monk called to him in a urgent voice, "Master, it is time for you to speak and the congregation will be waiting." Yogananda turned to him like a Santa figure with a wink in his eye and as he did so he said, "varoom, varoom," and sent a toy airplane grinding its way along to the dignified visiting monk who was also sitting on the other end of the balcony. He and Paramahamsa both offered up deep belly laughs and got up to go give their talks. The difference between the state they were in and the Monk's own state was itself the teaching, at least as the story was imparted to me by my analyst.

Paramahamsa Yogananda and his visiting dignitary were overflowing with child-like Christmas spirit and ready to share in its joyful and playful essence with the large audience who were by then very ready to receive it. It was a perfect and perfectly timed event from Paramahamsa Yogananda's state of consciousness in contrast to the monk's state of mind. That was why Paramahamsa Yogananda was master and the monk was the student.

It was Paramahamsa Yogananda, an Eastern Master, whose teachings and writings were ironically the ones that taught me how to properly worship and honor Christ, not the various ministers to whom I had been exposed over the years. His devotion to Christ and his joy with Christ in his writings and teachings moved me very deeply. It also empowered me to follow the natural leanings I had to surrender my heart joyfully, as I did when I was 'saved' by visiting missionaries several times in my childhood.

The importance of this story for me is that it resonates with my experiences, not only as a child, but also as an adult, of the playfulness and absolute delight of pure spirit. Yogananda's attitude toward his Christmas presentation was so perfect. The playfulness of the divine was not only visiting him, but also his guest, and was such an appropriate expression of the Christmas spirit. The freedom of play and laughter both embody the freedom of pure spirit. In Matthew 18:3 Christ is reported to have said, "Except ye turn, and become as little children, ye shall in no wise enter into the kingdom of heaven." As the spirit plays above, so the enlightened play below! This childlike wonder, awe and experimentation with inner space travel was present in my sky travel, nap travel and sleep travel as a child. My childhood experiences were validated as I was launched onto the spiritual path as an adult. The curiosity and joy of the ongoing discovery is itself part of the very nature of spirit.

My Childhood Experiences And Childrens' NDEs

WE GET SO MUCH pure joy and radiance from an infant or young child. There is so much playfulness in their spirit as they grow and change. It is as if they radiate the energy of a higher plane of existence from which they just came. Why shouldn't the heavenly side of the veil be a more expanded, more light-filled and more joyous extension of our experiences here? Matthew 6:10 says, "Thy kingdom come, Thy will be done on earth, as it is in heaven." Yoga scriptures say that the whole world is a play of that divine light. Jewish tradition says that we are made in God's image. Hermes Trismegistus (thought by some to be the Egyptian God Thoth), head of the Western Hermetic Tradition, brought us the understanding 'As above, so below'. It makes holistic sense that we experience certain dimensions here on earth of something that can be traced back through countless more subtle dimensions to a center dimension of pure light, fine enough and conscious enough to be called pure awareness, subtle enough to be present in everything, everywhere and blissful enough to make our heart smile at a sunset.

I would even say I <u>know</u> that it all fits together in a unified way. That is my experience of it. I experience the same light, upliftment, and joy in the writings of the saints of all of the religions I have contemplated. I can see no meaningful difference. When I do see a difference, it seems to me that it is probably in translation or interpretation. It was said of Ramakrishna, a holy man (whose birth, like Jesus and others, was forecast ahead of time and whose greatness was known before he was conceived or born) that he went on pilgrimages to many religions, practicing their methods and concluded they were in essence all the same.

One can particularly see the underlying unity in various religions and spiritual systems if one pays attention to the spiritual experiences of children. It is important to view these near-death and meditation experiences from a child-like point of view, setting our "collective conventions" thinking aside. It is even more interesting when a child reports a spiritual experience because, even though they may have had less exposure to the concept, their reports are similar to adult reports. There is a freshness and innocence in their honesty, which causes one to believe what they say.

Melvin Morse, along with Paul Perry, became fascinated by experiences of children who had died and were revived. His book "Closer to the light" is in part a wonderful compendium of reports of such children. He found that their innocent reports included all of the aspects of the NDE's of adults, only sometimes in more charming forms. As people familiar with the NDE literature will remember, the person who, in Dr Morse's words, "changed my life", was an eight year old girl, Katie, whom he was trying to resuscitate from a coma after nearly drowning.

Three days after a prayer session held around her by her family, she awakened from her coma. When she was interviewed by Dr. Morse she related to him that she had met the "Heavenly Father". She was led up a tunnel by "Elizabeth", who was "tall and nice and had bright golden hair." She was introduced to two souls waiting to take a body. She was given a glimpse, from her heavenly state, of her home and what her family was doing while her body was comatose in the hospital. She was then taken to the "Heavenly Father and Jesus". When the "Heavenly Father" asked if she wanted to see her mother again, she awakened back in her body. Her parents were of course quite astonished to hear her relate what they were doing while Katie herself was in a coma.

Before being influenced by Katie's story, Dr. Morse specialized in another unrelated area of medicine. Katie's experience, however, led him to set up a study of NDEs of children in his spare time, and eventually dedicate his life to such research. In his reports from that study, he discovered that other children had similarly remarkable experiences. One boy whose experience he reported heard a "whooshing" sound in his ears and then a buzzing when he traveled toward the light in his NDE. These sounds remind me of the sounds I would hear that I called my "buzzing" when, as a young boy, I expanded into an inner universe at nap time. This boy, however, as did so many of Dr. Morse's subjects, saw a light, which was like a "light bulb in his body". His experience of whooshing and buzzing also reminds me of an adult meditation of mine which was dramatically similar, though launched me into starry space. I will share that experience later in the Chapter entitled "The Third Eye Breakthrough".

Actually, it was a young boy named Ed to whose NDE I most related. He reported after recovering from a car wreck that he saw himself sitting between his parents with his face all bruised and battered. When sharing his NDE, he says, "But suddenly I began to float up and then everything became dark. Then I felt like I was speeding up. Soon I was traveling at a tremendous speed in total darkness. It was like I imagine space travel to be." He goes on to report a bright light filled with "love and knowledge" hanging over his head. Up to the point of the light, the feeling of speeding up and traveling in space was very similar to my boyhood experiences. At night, my expansions actually contained a luminescence, though not the powerful states of light reported by the children in the study. Those I would not experience until later in my life when I was a meditating adult. Dr. Eben Alexander's most blissful experience in his NDE, reported in *Proof of Heaven*, was expanding into the "core" as he named it, which itself was not white light, but was "...an inky darkness full to brimming with light," which he says "...is the home of the divine itself." Sharyn's blissful moments, too, were in a dark luminescence that was the divine, though she saw a brilliant light up and to the right that telepathically told her she had to return as she began to merge with it.

In general, the near death experiences of children reported in Dr. Morse's book seem to be more vivid and full of light than the natural meditations of my own childhood. Mine had luminescence but were more like the experience of one of the other children in the book who reported that a "glowing fog" separated him from the light towards which he was traveling. The children who had NDEs seemed to have more light filled experiences. The complete and utter absence of the body's distracting activities in NDEs is what, in my opinion, makes the NDE such an excellent prototype for meditations. But what would be our experience if we distill the essence of the NDE process and use it as a dharana, a meditation focus?

My childhood experiences, the night time experiences of the expanding walls and of walking toward the receding light switch, had elements of the OBEs also reported by a large number of the children in Dr. Morse's study. They often saw the doctors working on them, the layout of the operating room, and objects nearby. Though my eyes were closed at night when the walls expanded into space, I could see the layout of my room, the doors and windows where they actually were and objects in the room as they actually were. On the occasions in which I would catch up with the receding light switch, turn it on, and then find myself still immobilized in bed with the light off, I was obviously having an OBE. I had performed the task "out of body", or in other words, in my energy form, which felt the same to me as actually doing it, only without the desired physical results.

My childhood experiences were steps on a continuum, which would lead me closer and closer to encounters with The Light. They carry enough common elements of the childhood NDE's to cause me to speculate that there is a natural expansion of awareness towards a luminescence, which is full of "love and knowledge", as one of the children put it. With the body entirely out of the way (briefly dead), as is the case with NDE's, these experiences are extremely vivid and light filled. With the body only napping, sleeping, or engaging in focused visualization or imagination, such as the night sky experiences of my childhood, the whooshing, buzzing, and traveling in space sensations occur, along with the experience of a luminescence, but perhaps not with as much light-intensity, or at least without being able to see the light as clearly. I would like to know if other adults remember these natural expansions or out of body experiences of childhood like I do. I would welcome other's experiences and thoughts. I would guess it might be more common than we know. However, children might not find audiences who would take seriously these incredible and life shaping adventures into other realms. Who would believe them?

As I grew and matured as a child, the buzzing and space travel seemed to take different forms. My awe of the night sky continued. I remember one night walking home with a friend from the local Baptist church when I was 10 years old. We had attended an evening service with a visiting missionary who asked for sinners to come to the front to be saved. I had walked forward two other times when two previous visiting missionaries put out the call from the very same pulpit. I was saved each time. Each time I also experienced an expansion and a sense of joy in my heart. This night I walked forward with my friend to be saved because I liked the feeling it stirred up, particularly in this religious context. We talked all the way home about God and Jesus and what it meant to be saved. I shared with him about my "space travel" in the night sky. We discussed whether God and Jesus were up in that night sky. It was the first time I connected any religious meaning to my prior experiences.

We were very animated and so much in awe of the existence of a higher being who loved us so much. Being saved was such a high. We talked and talked and spun out all of the possibilities that followed from believing in God. Did he really watch everyone all of the time. How did he do that? Did he love bad people as well as good people? How could he? I got high again on these big questions. The answers weren't there, only the questions. But it was the questions that caused spirits to soar, just as when I lay on the grass staring at the heavens with questions, but no answers. My friend and I were really soaring with our combined questions!

We were also two of the best rock throwers in the 5th grade. We must have hit 80% of the telephone poles at which we aimed. We were cruising along with our feet barely touching the ground. Then, I was so inflated with it all that I took aim at the streetlight, which towered far over our short forms, and I hit it. And it shattered. And we deflated very quickly and ran home.

That night was very special. Somehow, talk of God, and more than that, questions about God, elicited the same expansion as the self-talk and questions about "forever" had elicited in that first experience I had with the night sky. That night with my friend a connection was made with the "forever" of space and the all pervasiveness of God. These things were part of a very special feeling and experience. They were tied together in some way. I understood this more and more when I would ask the same questions as an adult.

Other interests of mine at that time also connected me back to the expansion. I became interested in hypnosis. Another best friend and I got beginners books on the subject and began to practice on each other. His parents lived across the street from the church where I was saved three separate times. Their whole lives revolved around it. Ministers came and went over the years in the church, but his family was there to greet and say goodbye to each one of them. Their son was a bit of a rebel, like me, and even though his parents would have disapproved of our experiments with hypnosis, he and I repeatedly hypnotized each other and suggested to each other that we go deeper and deeper asleep.

As you might expect, when he hypnotized me, I fell deeper and deeper into expansion and "space travel" to his hypnotic suggestions. When he suggested I couldn't move my arm, I couldn't, because I was progressively more immobilized as I expanded into space and out of my body. I must have been an easy subject for him. He didn't seem to let go as much to my suggestions when he was my subject. However, we were both enthralled with the special powers that suggestions seemed to unleash. Magic, power, non-ordinary states; these unusual experiences are pretty heady stuff for a couple of kids. But if we could experience something extraordinary, then didn't it follow that something extraordinary existed?

Be Ye As Adults.....

ONE WOULD THINK THAT all of this early awakening and quickening of spirit would lead to an overtly spiritual adolescence for me, but that wasn't so. From high school through to my degrees in Psychology, I became too busy with the outer form of the "Hero's Journey" to spend much time in altered states. My states during this time were altered mainly by cigarettes and coffee, as I stayed up all night cramming for term papers and tests. I married young, had two wonderful children, worked and attended classes. Schooling went on and on since my goal became a doctorate.

During my undergraduate work at the University of Wyoming in 1959, my first wife's step-father asked me how I liked engineering, my dad's favored career path for me. I said, "it's fine," but he knew I was not sure. He said he saw college as a time to explore a variety of majors and he would support me in discovering what I wanted to do. I took that to mean financially and tried out four different majors before landing on a Philosophy/ Psychology major. I later learned that he didn't mean financially, though thankfully, I never had to test this and ask him for financial help because I worked my way through school, drew on Government loans, and received a small monthly amount from our parents. I'm glad I misunderstood his offer. That allowed me to spin an imaginary financial support net under us which gave me the confidence to follow my bliss, as the great mythologist of my time, Joseph Campbell, would urge everyone to do.

During one existential philosophy class, I remember learning the idea that God was an invention of humans to calm anxiety; the idea was that God was merely an opiate of the masses. I would argue vociferously with other students that seeking God was a sign of insecurity and weakness in a person. The outer rites of passage into manhood were so challenging that I think I needed to believe that a true hero simply persevered through hardship and obstacles until he prevailed, all alone on his own, as the existentialists viewed it. I tightened my seat belt and did what it took to succeed.

Though I took the support of existentialists, my first wife's stepfather's question launched me on a course of study which eventually led me back to the exploration of altered states! One humorous incident occurred after we were married. Several months after our wedding, she became pregnant and we moved to California to live temporarily with her stepfather and her mother until our first baby was born. Her stepfather, was a renaissance man. His doctorate was in Asian studies, his dissertation became chapters in a book on Sri Aurobindo, an Indian spiritual master, and he conducted weekend encounter marathons with his broadcast communications students at San Francisco State. He dropped LSD with Timothy Leary and helped start Esalen Institute near Big Sur. He was well read in Jungian psychology and when I was perusing his library, I came across a book whose title I read aloud: "Jung's Answer to Job". In my innocence, of course, I pronounced "Jung" with a "J" like "junk and a "ung" like "Rung". I also pronounced "Job" like "Bob" with a "J". He smiled in an amused way and said "well that is one way to pronounce it."

He died many years ago. He was the mentor who said to me "What do you want to do in life?" He gave my life back to me. I will always love him and be grateful to him. I shared with my ex-wife that I missed him and wished I had something to remember him by. She later brought me one of his books. It was "Jung's Answer to Job". She had remembered. I cried.

The seed he planted sprouted. I got my doctorate in Psychology and specialized in Jungian/Transpersonal work. As I mentioned in an earlier chapter, learned from a Jungian analyst who himself followed a spiritual master. I would ultimately attend literally hundreds of meditation and Jungian oriented workshops and a number of month long meditation trainings. I moved closer and closer to experiences of expanded states with each workshop I attended. The experiences I had of the inner realm as a child guided my journey as an adult, in spite of my attempts as a college undergraduate to deny it. My passion turned out to be that mysterious enchanted land of living myth, where altered states of consciousness, magic, transformation, and love, all prevailed over whatever set out to stifle them. I was ripe for new experiences in the realm of light.

The Medium Is The Message

MY FIRST EXPERIENCE AS an adult, which reminded me that a higher state of consciousness, a divine mind, existed, happened in my late twenties. It was an experience I had that once again awakened awe. This experience also raised some of those same old questions, which had initially led me into my first expansion into the night sky.

My first wife, Jane, and I separated in 1969. When we met at the University of Wyoming in 1959, we were both lonely and away from home for the first time. I saw her rehearsing in a college play and identified with her artist's spirit, replete with the strong inner life, uniqueness and air of mystery that I could not penetrate. We got married in our second year of college after a summer apart, shortly after returning to college. We both shared a frustration with the long, cold winters in our little basement apartment, the only windows in which were at ceiling level and were perpetually covered with snow. We would enter frenzied manias where we would say "lets move to California tonight and get out of here!!!" We chose California because her mother and stepfather, Richard Marsh, who changed my life with a question, lived near San Francisco and because a month and one half after our wedding she became pregnant.

There were many reasons we divorced 9 years later. A number of them related to getting married when we were so young. Some of them related to incompatibilities of temperament. However, I think my schooling and work took it's toll too, leaving her with two babies to raise, in the style of the time, with the father at school/work all day and too tired to help as much as was needed with the kids and house in the evening.

To the point of this chapter, after separating, we were seeing other people, but had not filed for divorce. Like many separated fathers, I saw my two children, a nine-year-old son with Cerebral Palsy, and a healthy six-year-old daughter on weekends. I awakened one morning when I didn't have the children with me, to a deep sense of depression. I was sure someone had died. I was so certain of it that I began calling around to my friends and relatives to discover who had died. One of my first concerns was the children, so one of my calls was to Jane. I told her about the sudden grief and depression descending out-of-the-blue and asked if the kids were all right. She said they were fine, but that she might know why I was experiencing those feelings. She proceeded to tell me that the day before she had filed for divorce.

I was stunned. That event matched the feeling of my grief and sense of depression. Something had died, not someone. I was not stunned by her filing for divorce; I knew that one of us eventually would. I <u>was</u> stunned because somehow, clear across the county from her, I began to grieve. How could that be true? I was aware by then that the brain/mind was an electromagnetic field, but I could never be convinced that it generated impulses strong enough to transmit across a county, particularly with the interference of a field of 1,000,000 other brain/minds, all radiating fields across the county in which we both lived. How could I distinguish her brain waves from anyone else's? It would be impossible a large county away.

There was an epiphany for me at that moment that there was a field of conscious energy, which acted as a medium for such apparent transmissions. There must exist a cosmic mind that knew what was transpiring in two distant places of it's mind at the same time. In other words, the same mind-stuff inhabited my wife and myself and the space between us (and beyond) knew, as each of us, something had changed. It was the only explanation that made sense. I could feel that old altered state from childhood begin to hum in me once more. I awakened once again to the awe of the great mystery. How does that higher state, with which we are apparently one, work?

My First Experience With The Light

SYNCHRONOUS TO THAT TIME when I awakened to a telepathic or clairvoyant feeling of depression in reaction to my wife's filing for divorce, I was introduced by a friend to someone she called the "Queen Bee" of West Coast psychics. Her name was Anne Armstrong. She turned out to be an ancient friend, an accurate seer, and psychic counselor who subsequently saw me through most major transitions in my life. She was my first spiritual teacher, teaching classes in psychic development and in meditation that Sharyn and I later attended on a regular basis. She passed away in 2010 and her husband, Jim Armstrong, has since finished publishing their book of spiritual adventures and channeled teachings, *Awakening the Divine Within*. I went to her to understand how I could psychically know about my wife filing for divorce, as well as sorting out how to process the finality of our married relationship and handling it with our children.

When I went to see her for the first time, I had no idea about what to expect. It was 1969 and I had come through the sixties, with all of its alternative ideas and life styles. She initially didn't fit my image of a psychic; She was no-nonsense on the phone, and lived in suberban Sacramento. But what did I know; she was my first. I was a psychic virgin. I learned later that she was so popular and had so many people making demands upon her that she had to be business-like on the phone. It was one of those hot, dry, summer days in that city. She greeted me at the door. I had driven several hours from San Jose and was perspiring and weary.

She certainly, however, looked the part of a psychic. She was an exotic, dark, Hispanic gypsy. I would later think that she looked like my image of a curandera, a Hispanic healer. She was slightly more personal in the flesh than on the phone and my interest began to be aroused. I began to be excited because, if nothing else, this was going to be an adventure.

She invited me into a bedroom made into a den where she obviously did all of her readings. She got a tape recorder ready. "At least," I thought, "she isn't afraid to commit her predictions and visions to tape. She must have confidence." She told me that she needed only the topic I wanted "read"; she would do the rest of the work. I began to be impressed. I told her that I was getting divorced and had somehow known about it psychically. I also wondered what was in store for me and my family. She closed her eyes, went inside, and released a long breath.

And then it happened. For me, the room became a pool of golden, liquid light, and my eyes were open, not closed. Then, as if a pebble had been dropped in the pool, three concentric rings of gold rippled outward from the middle of the room to the walls. My heart and the pool of golden liquid light seemed to be the same. I felt the ripple in my heart as well as saw it. She opened her eyes and looked at me. She said, "You are looking for a meditation teacher." My insides responded with a big "yes", though I had no idea at that time what a meditation teacher was or did. My energy leaped forward as if Santa Claus had called my name to come sit in his lap.

I knew she was right, but I wondered how she knew, when I hadn't even been aware of the need myself. At some level I must have known what a meditation teacher did. However, the last conversation I remembered having about that topic, I laughed at the person who mentioned meditation and said "Go to meditation classes for what - so I can learn to stare at my navel?" It was during that same time I was taking philosophy classes on Existentialism.

She asked me what I had just experienced. I told her about the golden rings of liquid light. She reaffirmed that I was looking for a teacher and gave me the name of one. She then closed her eyes again, went inside and gave me an accurate reading of my personality, the personality of my wife Jane, and why it was right we were moving on. My wife and I later went to her together for more guidance around our children through the process of divorce, especially our quadriplegic son. Periodically over the years we met with her to get her psychic help through major transitions with both of our children. She was so accurate and had such universal understanding. She reassured me one time that my daughter had a strong self-balancing mechanism that always brought her to balance with life. So far, I would say that has been true.

The liquid golden pond in Anne's room was my first adult experience of The Light. The recent movies where people are "morphed" into liquid silver or gold capture some of the experience I had that day. It was a direct and simultaneous experience/vision of my heart in some other dimension than my ordinary, everyday life. There was an exquisite and delicate pond of joy or ecstasy in my heart that I saw as a golden pond in my visual field. The ripples suggested that it was touched by something (Anne's energy?). In her presence, I had experienced an expansion into golden light that called to mind other vistas that I knew as a child traveler of the night sky.

Though the exquisite feeling/light combination was an addition to my childhood space travels, they were similar in other ways. There is a definite recognition at that point of my life of one in the other. By now, I was convinced that Anne was seated in a higher state of consciousness with its attending powers. She even earned more of my respect when she referred me to a meditation teacher in my area rather than convince me that only she could teach me. She wasn't just trying to build a clientele. The teacher to whom she referred me was an aikido instructor who also led a meditation group based upon the underlying principles of that ancient martial art. The referral was a perfect one for that time.

By now, I had learned three things: Expansion was (childhood experience). All pervasive consciousness was (knowing from a distance someone or something had died). Light was (my experience sitting in front of Anne Armstrong). My mind was beginning to put them together. There was a conscious state of light that was all pervasive and into which one could expand forever if he were but able to let go of his hold on collective reality. This was an earth shattering revelation for me. It was a direct experience of the meaning I would later learn to ascribe to the "Hanged Man" Tarot card: My reality had turned upside down. What I formerly believed was real was unreal. What I formerly believed was unreal was real. Hello figure/ground shift, my old cosmic friend. This time, though, I had the advantage of an adult mind with its improved capacity to put things together and analyze experience. This was, for me, a spiritual awakening and STE. Henceforth I would never allow myself to doubt it's existence.

Describing the Undescribable

As I SIT TO write today, I remember a story from Esalen Institute's oral archives. Esalen is a growth institute located on the beautiful Big Sur coast south of Carmel California, and the famous Pebble Beach Golf Course. Esalen, with hot tubs situated on a cliff overlooking arguably the most breathtaking coastline of the Pacific Ocean, was the alchemical laboratory for all of the "New Age" awareness techniques that would be explored by the pioneers of the 60's and 70's growth movement. The reader might recognize some of the growth leaders who ran workshops there, such as Michael Murphy, Joseph Campbell, Fritz Perls, the Halperns, Ada Rolf, Anne and Jim Armstrong, Bill Schutz (and his flying circus) and many, many more, not to mention my ex-stepfather-in-law, Richard Marsh, who helped get it started.

I call it the place where I teethed as a Psychologist. It was a magic school for me where I was introduced to sensory awareness, week long encounter groups, marathons and gestalt therapy. It was where I first was introduced to hatha yoga, zen meditation and creative dance.

The story I want to relate to you from the oral archives of Esalen Institute goes like this: A woman was arrested in a bus station as she was returning from Esalen. She had participated in a week long workshop there and had discovered, simply put, that she was God. This was not a narcissistic experience for her because she had also discovered that everyone else was God too. She was incredibly high on this experiential discovery, and as it turns out, perhaps a little inflated by it as well. She certainly didn't want to keep it to herself. In fact she wanted to shake everyone in the bus station into reality. "Don't you realize who you are?", she would say as she gently shook each one of them, smiling at them brightly with tears of joy in her eyes, "You are God! We are all God."

Evidently, there was a gap between her experience and theirs. Someone filled that gap with a diagnosis and the police took her to the nearest psychiatric ward, on a 72 hour hold, where she probably continued to try to shake people into reality. Such is the power of the first spiritual awakening.

It is probably a wonder that I myself wasn't hospitalized with the same diagnosis (Overcome by Spirit) in the late 60's and early 70's. After my experience of the golden pond with Anne Armstrong, I began exploring meditation with the aikido instructor to whom she referred me and also participated in all of the other experiential practices at Esalen Institute, including hatha yoga. I routinely spent time each day with these practices, completely inspired by my experiences with them.

One morning, before co-leading a growth group with a colleague, I performed my regular hatha yoga practice I had learned at Esalen Institute. This practice always calmed me down and gave my body a creamy feeling. On occasions, I would fall into an altered state filled with good feelings throughout my system. However, this particular morning, I tapped into an extraordinary, expanded state of absolute joy. I was as high as I had ever been on some inner energy field.

My group co-leader had come to my living quarters, which was a part of the growth center we had created in an old mansion/castle in Los Gatos California, the entrance of which is marked by the two huge cats that are the well known mascots signifying the meaning of Los Gatos, "The Cats". He joined me for breakfast before we co-led the group; but I was in a very altered state. I had the cosmic grin all over my face and was chuckling about everything I saw, thought, felt and heard. It was a good thing I was not in a bus station that morning!

He took one look at me and said, "I don't know what state you are in, but don't let anyone bring you out of it." In fact they couldn't have. A few hours into the group, a woman was sharing her pain, but all I could do was smile joyful smiles. She was crying and sharing and I was in joy and laughter at the play of it all. I didn't want to appear unempathetic, but I couldn't stop laughing at everything around me. It was all such a beautiful joke. She was playing her sorrowful role so magnificently. She and the rest of the group were "figure," and I had dropped into "ground".

As the woman became more and more angry with me, my co-facilitator kept her focused on her feelings toward me, using my position as a straw-man at which she could strike out at. He finally suggested she engage me physically, to express her frustration and anger, and had her push me. We stood up and locked hands at chest level and began pushing each other. She yelled angrily and I laughed uncontrollably. Finally, she snapped. She raged so loud that all of us began to laugh. Then, so did she. We were all rolling around on the floor holding our sides. The cosmic joke had won a round. We were so captivated by the humor of it all that as one stopped laughing, another would start. I finally put on a Beatles song, "Here comes the Sun", and we all danced ecstatically and sang along with the tape. As California-new-age as this sounds, it ranks among the mor profound experiences of pure spirit I have had.

The experience I was having couldn't be captured by words. There was such a gap between where I was and where everyone else was in the beginning. It took a physical, limit-pushing exercise to break down barriers to the experience, and even then, I'm not sure, nor will I ever be, that we all experienced the same state. It is possible that they began to laugh at me being so locked into that strange state. However I suspect at least a few of them were transported into the same or similar state that visited me that morning.

Just as Sharyn said about her NDE, words are limited when it comes to describing what can only be experienced. The fact is, there are no words I can write which would be powerful enough or descriptive enough to give you a taste of the experiences about which I have been writing. This is not because my experiences were so special. Most people I have spoken to who have stepped across the threshold to The Light share similar experiences and share the same frustration about the limited nature of descriptive words.

If I used words with the emphasis they would need to approach describing the experiences I have shared here, you would probably think I was exaggerating and being too poetic or too prone to "purple prose". Phrases like "Every cell of my body was filled with ecstatic, liquid, conscious light" probably sounds like a gross exaggeration to many people, but to the person who has had such an experience, these words might grossly understate the truth. The chasm between those who have had an experience of the other side, and those who have yet to have such an experience, is an enormous span.

Those who have not had such an experience tend to criticize those who have for exaggerating and mistaking some ordinary sensation for something extraordinary. However, those who have had true experiences of spirit can hold a righteousness about them that can really be a burr under the saddle of those who have not yet had such an experience. However, those who <u>have</u> had the experience were once also those who <u>had not yet</u> had the experience! Having been on both sides of the chasm, these people know just how big the chasm is and probably try too hard to recreate the awakening for their audience with superlatives. Unfortunately, those who have yet to find a way to have their own experiences of The Light can only know experiences from their side of the chasm. The other side, to them, is only imagination, which, for many, cannot be trusted or broached.

On the other hand, as my story of the alien tribe's sleep habits demonstrates, all of us participate daily in the magic of life but have too often been de-conditioned to viewing it fresh in each moment of our existence. If reflected upon, perhaps all of us would remember a moment where we experienced the other side. We may not have recognized it as such, but it may have a special place on the mantel of our inner fireplace. Perhaps the distance is a mental distance, not so much a real one. In fact, many widely known experiences may have their roots in The Light. Consider for a moment the phenomenon of falling in love.

Falling in love, the courtly love that Robert Johnson refers to in his book *We* began to occur in the Western world in the 12th or 13th century. It seemed to be one of the only socially acceptable ways in the West to open fully to one's heart. To dance and chant, as many other cultures do, until a divine experience is had, is not a part of mainstream western culture. There are exceptions of course such as some Jewish and Greek celebrations or the joyous singing of traditional hymns of inspired gospel choirs. But by and large, there were no rites or rituals that caused people to surrender to that wonderful state of bliss for which we all seem to yearn.

That all seemed to change, according to Johnson, as the people in the 12th and 13th centuries began falling in love. Troubadours would court married women, singing love songs under their windows until both were in a state of ecstasy. When they were both hopelessly entrenched in a state of love, or a state of "falling in love", the troubadour would move on, never consummating the affair, at least if he were one of the ethical troubadours. It was an affair of the heart only. And since it was so short lived and unrequited, it was intense and had a lasting impact on the lovers experience.

I was delighted to see Barbara Streisand's character giving a lecture on this topic in her movie, *The Mirror has Two Faces*. This "folie a deux", in history, answered the overwhelming need people had to lose their head in love. It is considered by some to be a primitive attempt to experience The Light. In all wisdom, we shouldn't judge the Troubadours or their ladies until we have tasted the "other side". If we have tasted it, we most probably will not judge them at all because we will understand that they are being moved by pure spirit and that falling in love can be a form of spiritual awakening that is projected onto one's romantic partner. Robert Johnson has written an entire book on the subject named, appropriately, *Ecstasy*.

Another piece of my writing I submitted for the book of poems, *We Are not just Daffodils* is relevant here. I called it *Love Sustained*:

LOVE SUSTAINED

Everything created was created out of Love. From the perspective of Love, all is transformed. Were we but to shift our awareness, struggling with the world of things would cease to exist, for the world, as we know it would cease to exist. The burdensome aspect of life is just a reflection of where we choose to invest our awareness. A simple shift towards love would change all.

New love is ambrosia that covers everything with its sweet glow. Just because it is hard to sustain, is it fair to say that it is an illusion and that young lovers must come to their senses and see reality? I don't think so. I think rather that such glorious moments when love is tender are themselves flashes on the True Reality, which, if sustained, would show itself to be our very own Self. Tune in to Love. Center yourself in Love. Make yourself ready for Love. The pains of Love are only growth pains, purifications of mind, body and soul for the Ultimate Reality.

When I wrote this, I was beginning to experience those rarified states of love. Those states themselves are the source of prose and poetic rendering, and to me are even more ecstatic than poetry and prose could ever describe.

Marion Woodman, a world renowned Jungian Analyst, shared in a National Film Board video entitled "Healing Spirit", an experience she had after being in an automobile accident. She was left with a ringing in her ear that would not stop. She was eventually driven to desperation by its persistence. Finally, at two o'clock one morning, she prayed for it to stop, or for her life to be taken. She had been praying like that for sometime; that is how desperate she was for the ringing to stop. She then describes an incredible experience that unfolded.

An orange rush of fragrance rose upward through her body from her feet to her head and upraised hands. She was drawn into a standing position with her hands stretched up high above her head. Every cell was transformed by the perfume until she had the experience she was the perfume. The feeling was one of pure spirit and she experienced herself as one with that spirit, not different from it. It changed her life completely. The ringing in her ears disappeared at that moment. She knew she had been healed by spirit and that God was not disembodied spirit, but lived in her very own heart. She describes the experience so poetically. It is the only way to begin to share it. One might be tempted to say she exaggerated to say she was "…one with spirit…" and that "…she was the perfume." However, the healing of a long standing ailment might suggest otherwise.

Though words generally cannot come close to describing how deep, exquisite and life transforming these experiences are, I think it is nonetheless important to continue sharing our experiences with words. We need to communicate in order to invite more and more people to come forward with their piece of spiritual reality, until we have a global patchwork quilt of spiritual experiences. When taken as a whole this global presentation of spiritual experiences might better circumnavigate the higher state we experience as God. The more critical mass we can develop on the planet with experiences of the light, the more people who have not yet discovered their own personal experience may be encouraged to seek their unique pathway to spirit. Then, what was background for them will become foreground and what was foreground will become background. Can you imagine the beauty of a world filled with awakened people? John Lennon could.

As inadequate as they are, words seem to be our only first approach to sharing what we have tasted. Genesis says: "In the beginning was the word and the word was with God and the word was God." This seems to be a reference to the principle that sound vibration does create, and written words are based on sound. They invoke subtle sound when repeated in the head of the reader. Silent repetition of prayers and mantras are based upon this principle. Ultimately we write in hopes that Spirit will stir in the background of readers minds and draw their attention inward towards the light, which can then illuminate the foreground of their experience too, showing it, as well, to be nothing but spirit itself.

Demonstrations from the Masters

AFTER SEEING ANNE ARMSTRONG for that first psychic reading and having my first intense experience of light, I began studying with the meditation teacher to whom she sent me. He was an aikido instructor. It was he who was teaching me at the time I wrote the article "Natural law and Psychotherapy" which appeared, along with pieces from other spiritually oriented writers of the time such as Alan Watts and Ralph Metzger, in *Geocentric Experience: A Bulletin*. In the article, I mention a number of the wonderful meditation exercises he taught us, some of which he would have us take into motion as aikido moves and some of which he would have us concentrate upon inside while sitting for meditation.

In a short time, I was formally meditating and was experiencing more illumination and expansion than I could handle. This man was incredibly advanced in meditation experience although he still had some rough edges as a human being. He taught me predictable access to fantastic universal states of light and peace.

I attended his aikido classes three nights a week. For those of you who may not have heard of this martial art, it was invented by a Japanese spiritual master named Professor Uishiba, or *O Sensei*, as his students referred to him. The stories about him are legend.

There were times where he held an open season on himself for all of his students. They were invited to attack and subdue him at any time they selected. They would jump out of the woodwork to throw him to the ground, only to end up on the ground themselves, sometimes not even knowing how it had happened.

One of the stories told by my instructor about his teacher allowing "open season" on himself by his students was that a student moved out of a bathroom stall and jumped at him while he washed his hands and brushed his teeth at the sink. The student grabbed his kimono sleeve, but miraculously was <u>not</u> thrown to the floor by his master. O Sensei's knowing was so subtle that he did not sense "attack" from the student. In fact, he was correct. The student was trying to save his master's kimono sleeve from the running water.

My instructor studied under this Master for a number of years and remembers one time going in for the attack on the practice mat and running into an energy field that disoriented him and turned him around. He then felt himself thrown to the mat by one finger of his master placed on his forehead. O Sensei used to say, "I am the Universe. Whoever attacks me attacks the Universe." Watching old movies of O Sensei being attacked and throwing his students around gives the impression that he was stating the truth. He was indeed established in a universal state of consciousness.

In my own aikido studies, two nights a week were spent attacking and tossing each other around in strict adherence to centered energy receptivity. We would sense the direction and force of the energy of our attacker, sense where he or she was going and then help that person land there. When done properly, it was the epitome of grace in motion. People flew toward each other like birds and were swooped up in the defenders' motions, gracefully landing on the mat or rolling up to a standing position. At its best, it was a dance of energy that was full of positive attitude, positive energy, and harmony. At its worst, it was powerful and would hurt if not surrendered to properly. If one held back, a roll would feel like a crash landing. If forced, someone would get hurt.

The third (evening) practice of the week we all went to the aikido instructor's house, which was a meditation commune for serious students, where he would guide us all into meditation. In meditation, he was miraculously sensitive to higher states of consciousness. As I grew in the light myself, I could progressively see an uncanny accuracy in his ongoing commentary about what was happening in any particular meditation. He would confirm my own experience again and again as he reported to the entire group what was happening in the group "space", during the meditation. Under his tutelage, I began to experience states of expanded light that had boundaries like the distant boundary of space I had imagined or seen in the night sky so many years before. Anne Armstrong had definitely sent me to the right place, at least for that particular time in my spiritual growth.

Although he made fun of people's need for a Guru, he himself acted like a perfect disciple of his sensei and subtly seemed to want us to revere him that way. I received what seemed like mixed messages from him. It was as if he were communicating to us "Act as if I am without formality. Treat me like one of a team (but the most special and gifted one of the team and the one on the team upon which all others must depend for every spiritual move they make)." The right question would bring his approval; the wrong question would bring cutting criticism and sarcasm. Pair that with my overly curious, overly sensitive, and often obsessive questioning/ responding and what you get is the ex-hood turned cop (which he was) tromping the mama's boy turned counselor (which I was). We each respected each other's sensitivity to other realms, but we couldn't have been more different in psychological nature, yet identical in our true basic nature!

When we would all sit for meditation, it was exquisite. In that world he was an extremely sensitive and tuned in teacher. One night we all sat, closed our eyes and began as we often did "sensing base". This was experiencing our lower body melt into a pool of energy that became more and more expansive, illumined, and divine. From this consciously grounded lower state, we would allow the upper body to melt as well and follow his directions as he guided us deeper into the group state of higher consciousness. My inner state soon began to expand on its own until I was being drawn into finer, more subtle states of being which at first activated my mind and then quieted it down with their glorious, peaceful, expanded, and luminous universal countenance.

One night as we all meditated together I experienced that I was expanding nicely within and around my entire body. I became aware of three huge balls of light entering my upper space, visible by the third eye in the region of the forehead. My instructor immediately announced to the group "We are attending a meeting upstairs." I then experienced three brilliant balls of light enter the group space, as if three beings of light had joined our meditation. He immediately announced "We have three visitors who want to exchange energy and information with us...relax, let go of heavy and sense finer." Then the inner space above my head brightened even more and I could feel the visitors each taking turns expanding us into several different types of states, each with its own thumbprint. I sensed one was more brilliant and clear. My instructor then said "sense clear." Then another of the illumined forms shone brighter with an incredible quality of all-pervasive love. Our instructor then said to the group "sense the heart space." The third illumined form expanded us all into a space of light that seemed formless. The instructor said, "How much can you let go of form."

After the meditation, others in the group shared that they had unusual experiences that seemed related to what he and I sensed happened. It was an incredible experience to have someone with his experience validate the subtle expansions of spirit and light that I myself was beginning to experience in the meditations we shared. I am filled with gratitude for his awareness of the subtle inner play of light and form and for his guidance in this subtle inner universe. His guidance found fertile soil in the boy/man I was, the one who had expanded, early on, into the dark of the night sky.

Background Comes to Stay

In THE EARLY 70's I was conducting a free class of relaxation and yoga mixed with centering exercises based upon the aikido/meditation instruction I was receiving. I was teaching hatha yoga in the format that I learned at Esalen Institute and I was using the building that hosted the crisis center that I set up and was directing at that time. One of my students informed me that Ram Das (formerly Richard Alpert, partner with Timothy Leary on the early LSD experiments) was introducing a Guru from India in Santa Cruz just miles south of where I lived. "Why don't we go over and see them both?", she asked. I said yes. I think I and all of the class members who went were more interested in seeing Ram Das, because he was our local spiritual hero.

By then, my meditation instruction in the aikido classes included a joint meditation exercise where we would sit with a partner and meditate on our own expansion of consciousness and sense that our partner was doing the same until a merging was experienced of both states into one. At the introductory program, Ram Das had come out on stage and warmed the group up for this visiting Guru by having us sing *Amazing Grace* and other spiritual hymns and chants. I decided to test this new master in town by doing a partner meditation with him even though I was in the audience and he was on stage.

This Guru was quite a character, wearing saffron robes, speaking in Hindi, stroking his shaved head, making points with his hands, and pointing up a lot. I closed my eyes, went inside, and watched my inner state expand, brighten, and generally intensify and practiced sensing that his energy state was a mirror to mine. I did feel the Higher Self was showing itself and it did seem that the state of the Self in this unusual swami (or the room in general) was very clear, intense, and expanded. I left the program thinking he was probably the real deal, having had no feeling of in-authenticity about him.

The translation was mediocre, but the gist of it aligned with the aikido teachings - that there was a vast intelligence behind all of creation that could be sensed and merged with, given the quality and steadfastness of our own focus upon it. Concentration led to merging with it and ultimately we realized we were it. What was different in what the master said, as contrasted to the aikido teachings, was that a master could awaken the spiritual energy and guide the students progress from inside, leading the student ultimately to recognize within himself the state of enlightenment the master is in.

After seeing this visiting master and about the same time as the aikido meditation with the three visiting teachers (from inner space), I saw an expansion of my inner world that I can now say became permanent. I was meditating three hours a day then, half in the morning and half in the evening, and every time I closed my eyes, I literally saw a rounded universe of light as far as my inner eye could gaze. The ongoing, seemingly endless, expansion seemed to be experienced directly too, to the North, the South, the East and the West as well as the above and the below of it all. It had a subtle contour like the boundary of space in my childhood sky-staring but was of such a shimmering, radiant quality that I literally glowed inside. This expanded state seemed to be a living consciousness, showering me with grace, with insight and with bliss.

I just came across an experience written about by Jeffrey Long, M.D. in his book *Evidence of the Afterlife* that confirms the similarity between my meditations and NDEs. He writes, "Many NDErs indicate they have 360-degree vision during their experience, sometimes even more than that. The term 360 degrees refers to two dimensions only, while NDErs often report spherical, three-dimensional visual awareness simultaniously in all directions - forward, backward, right, left, above and below." I think I know just what the NDErs mean when they report that. Sharyn also talked about her ability to see in all directions without seeming to change focal points while traveling toward the light.

During my meditations, the "Third Eye", as it is called, seemed to have been permanently opened, at least to a certain level of vastness and light. It would reflect the activity in all aspects of that expanded state. Out of that lasting expansion of light a host of beings of light would continue to approach, each bringing their own teaching, not in the form of thoughts, so much, but in the form of qualities and colors and various degrees of light and expansion representing different states of being.

To this day, I am not sure how much of this expanded awakening to attribute to meeting the master that Ram Das was introducing, and how much this might be the natural path of the aikido instructor's guided meditations (or both). I only know that chronologically the higher, luminous state made a permanent home in me right after meeting the traveling master and has been constantly available to my inner vision and experience since that time. I also know that when I described the painful neck sensations and the draw upward into inner space, my aikido/meditation instructor seemed not to know what that meant, while the master, whom I spent years with later, chuckled at my concern and taught techniques that eventually lightened those pains. When he said a true guru can awaken and guide the devotee's inner journey into higher states it seemed to be true for me. My tune-in to him and his state must have expanded my meditations.

One night during this time period, I sat in meditation for around two hours before going to bed. Whenever I do that, I seem to prime the pump for OBEs. This one stands out because of the difficulty I had re-entering my body. I was dozing off after going to bed and was pursuing the continuing expansions begun in the meditation. Falling asleep, I could count on my awareness expanding, intensifying, and moving for an hour or so through state after state, differing in degrees of expansion, of light, of love, of peace and of so many other combinations of divine qualities. I never wanted to miss any of these and so it often took a long time to fall asleep.

As I mentioned, there was an expansion of my "Over-Self" happening above my head, similar to a hot air balloon pulling all my consciousness upwards, that put great pressure on my shoulder and neck muscles and tendons, which tended to keep me awake late into the night. The stress was what I now consider a "guarding reaction" of my forehead, neck, face and shoulders to the expansion and intensification of my inner state. In particular, I was reacting to the newly experienced movement up into what in yoga is considered the Sahasrara at the top of the head (often represented on statues of buddhas as the thousand petal lotus at the top of the head).

It is not different from the guarding reaction which athletes experience to pulls and sprains, where the muscle groups around the injury tighten to protect the injury but can themselves spasm from their extreme contraction, putting vertebrae and ribs out of place and causing their own injuries in muscle tissue. As my energy ballooned above my head, my body from the shoulder blades up would be in pain too; the "Agony of the Ecstasy". Ecstasy equals pain became conditioned into my psyche. I still have this reaction, but it has attenuated as I have learned to relax and have dropped some pounds of flinching ego.

Getting back to the experiences of this night, sometime after I dozed off, I noticed that I was awake. I saw a white strap hanging from the beamed ceiling above me. I literally, or as literally as one can in another dimension, pulled myself up and out of my body with it and hovered over my body. I also felt my body become paralyzed. I was in both places at once. The paralysis was familiar to me by now from my childhood expansions. The similarity was there, too, in seeing my room as it was from another dimension, which the reader might remember when the walls of my childhood bedroom would seem to expand outwardly towards infinity.

However, there were differences between my present bedroom viewed from this out of body dimension and the same room as it was viewed in my waking state. In this OBE, I saw a couple sitting at a table that was over my meditation table. Their table was a regular kitchen type table and they were enjoying a meal. My meditation table was a large trunk, lower than their table, fitting under it. I approached them, but they kept on eating as though they couldn't see me in the diffuse form I was in. I remarked to myself that they must live in my house too, only in another dimension. I wondered if the energy where I meditated had anything to do with their choice of location for their kitchen table, or vica versa.

Then an even stranger event occurred. A beautiful nymph appeared to the right of me. I turned, and much like Odysseus experienced with the sirens in the Odyssey, I listened to her sensuously sing a hypnotic refrain in a soft whispery voice, "Little pearl, in the sun, little pearl I'll get you one. Little pearl, in the sun, little pearl I'll get you one." Unlike Odysseus in Homer's Odyssey, I hadn't strapped myself to the mast of my ship. I began to follow her into the darkened second bedroom of my cottage on the hill. As I followed her into the dark, I became spooked. To this day, I don't know if she was seducing me into some strange realm of consciousness or whether she was an angel guiding me into a particular state of light.

Dr. Alexander related in his talk that he found himself being led out of a muddied state of consciousness he first arrived at in his NDE by a beautiful feminine presence. He followed her where she led him and she did show him higher states of the divine consciousness. She even turned out to be a sister he never got to know in his earthly life who had died earlier on. It is interesting that Sharyn pointed out to me that I too have a sister who died a short time after birth. It makes me wonder.

Yoga scriptures describe a tiny blue pearl that comes into one's meditations and, when focused upon, can open one into a blue state of consciousness that in the Hindu tradition is considered the highest state this side of formlessness. I sometimes regret that I didn't stay with my "siren" long enough to find out what she wanted to show me. The increasing darkness was too much for me to handle and I, as body, tried to get up.

However, as I tried to get up in order to wake up (if you know what I mean), I couldn't strain hard enough to get soul to join with body. It just wouldn't happen. I panicked. I tried three or four times harder than the times I forced myself awake as a child, when the walls began their expansion into infinity. I was still hovering above the bed out of my body, in spite of my attempts to move. I was still both hovercraft and land vehicle, soul and body. I would try to will myself awake to draw the soul back into the body, and simultaneously, I was also the soul hovering about, glad to be free of the body. I can understand the higher need to be unconfined, but I was also a panicked body/mind that needed to feel inhabited. Of course, why would a hovering soul want to enter a straining, panicked body? It was a "Catch 22".

Then I had to go to the bathroom. I was so glad to discover that I could finally walk into the bathroom, turn on the light, and urinate. I felt the release, and then went back to the bed. Then I felt the urgency to urinate and realized that I was still out-of-body and had performed that little ritual virtually! I repeated this several times, being convinced each time that I had actually succeeded. I finally had to go so badly that I did force myself up, little by little (move the finger, move the head, move the arm, move the leg) until I could sit up. My body felt like it was that of a running back after a football game. I was stiff and felt like I had been beaten up. It was like a nightmarish Aikido match where I stiffened when I should have flowed, rolled like a square wheel, and then landed on all of my pointed joints.

I was a mess that day. I obviously didn't earn even amateur standing with this universal expansion business. I didn't pass my astronaut's test. And yet I was launched on an unending space voyage where I would have to learn to pilot an expanding universal spacecraft that was totally out of my control. If the Charioteer in the Tarot deck signifies successfully commanding the instincts to obey, using the invisible reins of thought, then, as the journey into higher consciousness is commenced, I seemed to be more like Icarus. In the myth of Icarus, he as a young man had grabbed his dad's chariot without a thought given to the power it contained and the dangers that it could produce with its great speed. For those yet to encounter this myth, Icarus has no control over such power, drives his dad's chariot too far and too fast, ending up too close to the sun, which melts his wings and sends him plummeting into the ocean (of the unconscious) where mythologists say he must master the forces which will strengthen and mature him into the man who can control the chariot like his dad could and as does the charioteer in the Tarot deck.

Even though I was frightened and humbled by the altered states that seemed to have their own mind and went about their own play, this and many later experiences similar to it, were still only small glitches in the electrocardiogram of my spiritual life. They soon fell into the "what an adventure" category of my thinking, though my body has carried a waxing and waning pain from the friction between the absolutely free spirit and the too often contracting emotional and bodily nature I seem to have earned this time around.

OBE experiences such as the ones I have shared with you seem to engage the traveler in many different vacation spots, not all of them heading for the light. It is also true, though, that not all NDEs are directed towards the light either. The similarities in the OBE travel associated with awakened states that naturally flow out of meditation practices and the OBE experiences connected with NDEs seem to be the sense of travel, of expansion, of moving into altered states of consciousness, as well as glimpses of the body at rest in some room or on the ground, while the soul is traveling and expanding. I think once the soul is set free from its usual identification with body/mind/emotions, it is free to soar within the body as meditation, and outside the body as the various and strange OBEs both NDErs and meditators have experienced.

Confirmation of the Third Eye Breakthrough

ABOUT A YEAR INTO my meditations with my akido/meditation instructor and around the same time I was introduced to the Indian Master by Ram Das, I was also introduced to the book *Autobiography of a Yogi*. The incredible experiences of Paramahamsa Yogananda, a spiritual master from India, who penned the book, were so much like what I sought, and to some extent had tasted, that I cried in recognition all the way through the book. Paramahamsa Yogananda was such a great and loving being. He had so much respect for Christ and the other spiritual masters in his lineage. He was even more devotional than I felt inside. Paramahamsa taught a form of yoga meditation that seemed quite similar to the teachings of the Indian master introduced to me by Ram Das.

One story that might be of interest here happened as I was searching for the cottage I mentioned in the OBE above. I had looked in the newspaper ads for a cottage in or near Los Gatos which is at the southern edge of Silicon Valley. I simultaneously was looking for a Paramahamsa Yogananda meditation center in the area hosted by SRF (Self Realization Fellowship), which was his spiritual foundation.

After a month or so of looking in the classifieds, I finally decided that I would advertise my need for a cottage and let a landlord find me, since I wasn't having much luck with the meager listings in the classifieds. To my delight, someone called and said there was a cottage on top of a hill in Los Gatos. Would I come up to see it? He gave me directions and I immediately started up the winding road excited at the prospect of finally finding my new home. As I began searching for the driveway to the cottage, which turned out to still be a quarter of a mile ahead, I saw a sign on the immediate right that said **SRF** in big letters. You can imagine my double delight! I was guided to both in one trip. With the odds of that happening by chance, it would be hard not to see divine intervention at work.

Synchronicities like that run chills up and down my spine. This synchronicity was thrilling. Needless to say, I rented the cottage and attended the center. The cottage was home for one of the most intense periods of my formal practice of meditation and was the place where I deepened my love for Paramahamsa Yogananda, his teachings, chanting and meditation. I attended both the SRF center near my cottage and one in downtown Los Gatos. Another divine arrangement was that I would often see one of the main teaching assistants of the aikido/meditation group at these SRF meetings and we would compare notes about the two spiritual paths.

It was in this cottage that I pulled away from the life of a divorced man in a singles apartment complex and walked into a life more like that of a monk. I read and reread *Autobiography of a Yogi*. I was still practicing Aikido meditation, had experienced an awakening that was probably from another Indian master, but was now chanting Self Realization Fellowship chants and reading and following Paramahamsa Yogananda's teachings as well. At that time, I accepted him as my spiritual teacher, my guru. Since he had passed on and wasn't available for direct physical contact, I would imagine that an enormous Eucalyptus tree that towered over my cottage was Paramahamsa Yogananda himself and would pray to the tree and meditate on my destiny. Was my destiny to be a monk? If not, what role should I play in life? Should I become a spiritual teacher? If so, should I become a yogi or an eclectic, drawing from Aikido, Yoga, Transpersonal Psychology and other paths as well?

Paramahamsa Yogananda saw Christ as one of the avatars; born-enlightened teachers, at the beginning of his lineage of self-realized masters. This satisfied a deep connection I felt to Jesus Christ and the path of the Christian monk. I shed many a joyous tear in contemplation of the figure of Christ, and now that included Paramahamsa Yogananda's own devotion to him.

So there I was, a Japanese martial arts student turned yogi with a Christian monkish flavor, meditating 3 hours a day and also following the Jungian dream path in therapy with a Jungian Analyst who also had a spiritual master who just happened to be Paramahamsa Yogananda! Sounds pretty California-new-age as I reflect on this part of my journey! My favorite story about how California became populated is that the United States was turned on its Western edge and all of the "loose pieces" fell down into California. My own spiritual path might add credence to that explanation!

In looking back, I think I was trying to pull together a path for myself that would lead me on my own particular journey and become my own unique pathway to enlightenment. I studied Paramahamsa Yogananda's teachings for two years and deepened my practices of his yogic way. He received devotion from me that I didn't know I had. I also pursued aikido based meditation and actually had some of my more expansive and intense experiences with this meditation teacher and his group of students. In retrospect, I think I experienced an awakening from the guru Ram Das introduced that evening, who out-shined all of the others as was evidenced by the chronology of my expansion into the upper regions after meditating on him. I was also reintroduced to him (without my realizing it was him) 4 years later by one of my colleagues, the synchronicity of which underlined him as the Guru for me, whom I have followed since. I believe I received the awakening this guru explained called Shaktipat Initiation: the powerful awakening of spiritual energy in the seeker by the Guru's own higher state.

As an aside, though my involvement with the SRF center of Paramahamsa Yogananda had ended 40 years ago, I recently walked into an antique store in Petaluma, California and was reintroduced to his influence. The town's main street is a throwback to the 1950's and was used as a backdrop for movies like *American Graffiti* and *Peggy Sue Got Married*. It was also favorite antiquing territory for Sharyn and myself. I was gazing into a stall in one of the antique collectives and saw two matching, elegant, expensive, Victorian picture frames. My gaze was first drawn to their beauty. Then I noticed the pictures that were in the frames. I became transfixed. There, in that unusual and unexpected setting, was a pair of carefully and gorgeously framed pictures of Paramahamsa Yogananda and his guru Sri Yukteshwar. I had evidently stumbled onto some wealthy devotee's loving tribute to his Guru. Some relative must have sold items from the estate with no knowledge of the spiritual implications of the pictures. As it turned out, no one at the store was aware of the significance of the pictures either. They simply wanted to sell the frames.

The instant I recognized the pictures, a thick cloud of universal love engulfed me and I dropped into a deep state of peace on the spot. My wife had a hard time getting the dazed smile off my face the rest of the day so I could relate to her and our getaway weekend. It was another synchronicity that happened in relation to Paramahamsa Yogananda. I had once again received the grace of that great master. Needless to say, they now hang in my meditation room along with the pictures of other Masters important to my journey.

One meditation practice Paramahamsa Yogananda taught was to focus the gaze in the area of the third eye, the space between the eyebrows. People of India and other places honor the third eye with a red dot, or smudge between the eyebrows. It is the location of one of the energy centers called chakras that reside in the energy body that animates the physical body. The chakras are gateways to the experience of higher states of con-sciousness that are the embodiment of different qualities and are connected to the earthly realm as well. For example, the first chakra, located at the base of the spine, which is named the Muladhara Chakra, connects us to instincts such as territoriality and survival impulses, but also grounds our meditations when activated and focused upon. The third eye, which is the sixth chakra, is called the Ajna Chakra, and has to do with our capacity for spiritual vision and related abilities.

I was living in the cottage at the time, but spending the night at a friend's house. I had a difficult time getting to sleep in that new situation, so I decided to meditate on the space between the eyes with my eyes closed, just as Paramahamsa Yogananda advised in his teachings. Whenever my mind would wander, I would bring it back to this focus. At the rate my mind wandered, this was necessary about every 10 seconds, . Little did I know that I had begun what became an all night vigil.

I realized later that I used a diffuse, relaxed gaze in my concentration on the Third Eye this night, much as I did at nap time as a child. In an the next eight-hour period, I returned again and again to this focus as my mind wandered to fantasized encounters with the Aikido teacher, with other people in my life, with my work, with my imagined spiritual future and many other things. I can't possibly convey how busy and cluttered my mind can be. If I can learn focus then anyone can learn focus!

Anyway, that night was focus, focus, focus, again and again and again and again. At first, I just wanted to close down my mind before sleep and fall asleep in a nice meditative space. However, my mind would wander to some worry and I would have to refocus on the third eye space. Repeatedly my mind would wander to some past, unresolved experience and I would need to refocus. My mind would then turn to some dream or desire and I would once again refocus on the third eye. The ease of focus in my child-hood naps embarrasses me as an adult!

As my concentration improved that night, I could simultaneously feel the pattern of expansions and brightening of inner space to which I was growing accustomed. With this continual reinforcement for my efforts, I was able to keep this refocusing practice going all night. As the space brightened, I would concentrate more. As I concentrated more, the space would brighten. The light of dawn itself was just around the corner. This early morning soft blue darkness is a special and quiet time to meditate. It was then, near the end of the eight-hour period, that a strange thing hap-pened.

My first perception was that the bed had begun to vibrate. My entire forehead was vibrating and in the beginning, I didn't have a clue as to why. It did not dawn on me at first that the meditation practice was producing the effect because the effect was too physically real. For a fleeting moment, I suspected that the alarm clock had fallen on the bed and was muffled and vibrating near my pillow!

Then the vibrating became more and more localized inside of my forehead. My entire frontal brain was vibrating. This was definitely not the alarm clock. And then as suddenly as it began, it changed into a whoosh and I was on my way. I was literally drawn like air into a vacuum through my third eye. The whoosh was a vibrating whoosh that sounded like air passing through a tight tube.

Then I was in space. I was as certainly in space as I experience myself being in ordinary life. It was an illumined space but still a nighttime space. This inner sky was a glowing soft dark blue all around, like the outer night sky must have been between dusk and dark as a kid, and the stars and the moon were shining brilliantly as I soared like a satellite through all of their glory and splendor. Then I became aware of something huge floating in that space with me. It was as large as the Star Ship Enterprise appears to be in the beginning of the Star Trek episodes. It was a huge titanium or platinum circle and square, created as one huge sculpture in space. I knew intuitively it represented the Yin and the Yang, the masculine and the feminine, inextricably joined and yet unique in each individual magnificence. I had broken through to a place where Yin and Yang appear to be one. This was a glimpse, and an expanded experience, of the principle I knew from studies of the dynamic tension between opposites that lies behind creation. This must have been a direct experience of what Jung wrote about as the universal realm of archetypes.

The state I was in, and of which I was a part, was incredible. I was completely free. I was in the state my wife Sharyn described in her NDE as the state "…everyone yearns for." I was floating free with an experience of infinite space. I was being shown the absolute harmony of the universal whole. The message was the medium, the state of consciousness itself. The symbol was of the experience and was not different from the experience. Just as the square and circle were one, so I was one with them, their harmony, and the harmony of the expanded state of consciousness itself. This was another situation where words fall short in describing the experience.

This experience of the yin yang symbol also reminds me of the little boy named Ed, whose NDE I mentioned before. The whoosh, the travel, the night sky, the experience of space, and the feeling of peace he had, were all mine too. In fact, it was as if it were my very own nature that I was experiencing, not some foreign state of mind. I was at complete peace for an extended period of time and then my curious mind began to pester the experience with its questions. What did I do to get here? How can I continue it so I can be in that space forever? Am I still focusing on the third eye? Is there more here to experience and learn? Is this God? My questions began to draw my mind into "figure" in the figure/ground relationship, and I soon began to return to a more physical reality and became aware of lying in bed, though I was still in a special state of mind.

I stayed calm and quiet for another hour and then had to get up to go to work. Even though I had not slept, my day was rather effortless. I felt a little strange - similar to the state of consciousness St. John refers to as, "In the world but not of the world". It was strange because it was new. I now recognize it as a state of spiritual detachment that we are capable of as we spiritually mature. This detached state is mentioned in a number of different scriptures and is part of most spiritual traditions. I now know from experience that detachment is a loving and blissful state, and not some dry detached state that the word conjures up in the English language. I found that state so different from waking life that there was a simultaneous tendency that day to either stir up some form of excitement or to begin to move energy around in some way so as to feel and appear more "normal". My oh-so-human mind was not ready to accept the experience as a desirable permanent place of residence for itself.

The mind that had to refocus for eight hours straight in order to have a breakthrough was also the mind that predictably began to scatter to all directions of my everyday world, and, for a long time after that, I could not conjure up so dramatic an experience, even in my deepest and longest meditations. It was not until an Easter some years later that my meditation experience once again paralleled the NDE experience in many respects, and at that time I discovered that within the smallest point resides the entire universe.

The Infinite Point of Light

AN EXPERIENCE OF ILLUMINED states of consciousness, that began to help confirm my spiritual worthiness, occurred during one of my efforts to break through to the divine during one of the Christian holidays. I have always had strong devotional feelings for Christ and his story. This experience happened on Easter of 1974. Since the Easter celebration was nearing its culmination the next day, I wanted to appeal to Christ (Christ Consciousness) as the guru of the occasion, to fill me with its grace. I was feeling the gratitude in my heart for such a loving and sacrificial path that we are taught Jesus took for us all. We are taught to approach the "Father" through dedication to the "Son" or as more mystical traditions suggest, approach the "Absolute" through the "Enlightened Master", each of whom is "the Son (or Daughter) of God".

In Eastern philosophies like Hinduism and Yoga, the "Son or Daughter" isn't Jesus the person, but "The Christ", the enlightened state of the master, that has always been present for mankind's spiritual evolvement. The "Son or Daughter" is the role spiritual masters commonly play in relation to the "Absolute", who is considered the "Father", though there are other roles for the deciple to assume too such as the divine lover, the humble servant, the perfect student and so on. It was decided hundreds of years after Jesus's death by the body politic of some of his more organized followers that he must have been teaching that he, Jesus, the man, was the only way to God. This has never made any sense to me because there were so many thousands of years of people finding God before Christ's appearance through so many enlightened teachers who provided awakening and guidance. I imagine that many of you, like I, find it difficult to imagine that for all of history God sent only one enlightened being through which we could know God, at only one particular time in history.

At any rate, that year I approached meditation the Saturday before Easter with special feelings in my heart and the determination I would meditate that night until I experienced Christ. That was my goal. I knew that it would take self-effort paired with grace, and while I wasn't sure about whether I was worthy to be graced with such a divine experience at that particular time, I was determined to do my part. I was committed to make heroic self-effort inspired by saints I admired like St. Francis of Assisi. Raphael Brown, writes in *The Little flowers of St. Francis of Assisi* that St Francis fasted and prayed for 40 days and nights as Christ had, but ate a half loaf of bread during this time so as not to outdo Christ, his master, in austerities.

I sat, closed my eyes and performed a centering practice. I sensed my lower body melting into a more expansive state of liquid light. For the first hour of the meditation, I deepened my concentration and that deepened the peace of the state I was in, which began to open gateways to shifts in intensity and brightness of the inner spaces I visited. I would pray intermittently for Christ to bless me with an appearance, a sign, an experience. I would then increase my focus, lighten my attitude, let go of distractions and melt as much as I could into delicate holograms of light. The holograms would start as a shimmering shift of awareness and then power up as if they were each an electromagnetic field that would finally draw me into their fullness with a force that my body would slightly resist, as if they were a threat.

My body seemed to be reacting to a sensation that it might have interpreted as "devouring". I felt that if I could but let go of this guarding reaction, then the sensation might morph and be experienced in a more positive light (pun intended) as a shift to higher states of consciousness. Evidently, to the extent we are attached to normal body/mind/emotion consciousness with all of its flinching at sudden movements, we can feel as if we were being swallowed up - or devoured - by something much larger than ourselves. In fact, in a sense this is true, but we learn later we are being consumed by our own "Self"! For me, "mastering" these shifts has become the exact opposite of control, which the word "mastering" seems to imply.

These shifts don't seem to be totally under my conscious control so "mastering" them might be more accurately described as surrendering to them. However, to take charge of surrendering is to not surrender! I think a very high form of paradox exists here where the interaction of Grace and self-effort finally must merge or converge into surrender. What a subtle and mysterious process this is. To this day, I get caught in this inner conflict. I cannot yet say that I am an expert at surrender because I still bump into that paradox, which means I am still in my mind at that point. I have, though, had glimpses of <u>being</u> surrendored as will be clear later in this chapter.

As the states of light began to demand surrender in my Easter meditation that night, I received visuals that were of stone structures similiar to castles or ancient monasteries. The rooms of light into which I would be drawn were rooms with stone walls. There were long stone walkways along the stone buildings with columns supporting a sloping roof over the walkways, much like the old missions. The light illuminating the rooms was otherworldly. It might begin with a speck of light in the distance, which would approach me, gathering size and brilliance as it neared. At the last moment, when I knew it would engulf me, or more descriptively, draw my consciousness into itself and merge my consciousness with its own, I would see a monk-like face in gossamer light marking the brilliant presence of that being's quality or countenance. I thought I recognized a few of them such as Saint Francis who is in fact one of my favorite saints. Others in the parade of lights I was to witness, I didn't recognize. They appeared in robes of brown or white and at times had clear faces and at other times manifested just-forming faces that were not clear by the time their particular quality of light engulfed me. It seemed I was visiting celebratory gatherings.

I found that there were subtle differences in the qualities, colors and feeling of the states with which I would partially merge. Each seemed complete within itself, needing nothing other than what it was. However, while one seemed full of pervasive compassion, or at least stirred that quality in my heart, another seemed to be ancient wisdom personified. It wasn't that words of wisdom would be imparted to me. It was as if the state was the personification of wisdom. It was wisdom. As it, I would see all things clearly. It seemed to me that the teaching was the state (once again, the medium is the message). It was reminiscent of the visiting masters meditation I mentioned earlier. The highest teaching may not be a word whispered into one's ear, but a state of consciousness gifted one by that consciousness.

It was early Easter morning by now, about 4:00 A.M. I was feeling filled with the visitations and the qualities each visitor imparted. I was also aware that my goal might not be reached. I had been graced throughout the night with meditative states that seemed to be the celebration of Jesus's great surrender to his destiny and his resurrection as a being of light. It seemed to me that many great beings were also celebrating the same event and I had been allowed to taste their states of being as they worshipped the occasion. What more could I want?

Then, with a surrender of my efforting, an acceptance of the fruits of that night of prayer and meditation, and an acceptance that it was the end of my meditation, the tiniest pinpoint of light appeared in my visual vista. At first it seemed like another celebrant, however I soon sensed that this one was different. It was of the purest golden/white. It was a small seed of light. I became utterly fascinated with its beauty. I relaxed my gaze rather than sharpening it. Relaxing it sharpened it. I was enraptured by the beauty in that little point of light. I could also feel that it had a more powerful draw connected to it, similar in concept to my understanding of the workings of a black hole in space. It was as though this light had its own gravity! All of my attention was being drawn into it.

As incredible as it seems, I felt my entire vast consciousness being sucked into a tiny point of light. I knew, as an expanded state of consciousness, I wouldn't fit. It was sci-fi in action. There was no way that I could resist the pull, such was the tremendous power of the gravity. It was just as amazing to me that my expanding state could be drawn into such a small point so easily. As I type this, I remember a silly demonstration by a character in a T.V. movie who drew a dress fabric through a finger ring to test whether it was silk. No matter how much fabric was tested, it could be drawn through the ring if it was silk! I guess expanded consciousness can be drawn through a small ring if it is truly the silk of consciousness.

I was forced to surrender at this point in my Easter experience. Maybe the final act of surrender is actually an act of grace; we are surrendered! In a very short time the point of light consumed me. Entering it was, and continued to be, an exquisite experience. It was as if that tiny point of light was the end point of all experience; it was the final destination. Once I entered it, I felt I may not return and didn't seem to care one way or the other (this sentiment was expressed by Sharyn in her NDE). I was in some kind of heavenly state representing Christ. Perhaps this is similar to the NDE experience some people have experienced by merging with the light at the end of their perceived tunnel.

Immediately upon entering the point of light, however, my consciousness expanded and merged with what, from the inside of that point of light, turned out to be a vast universe of brilliance. It was the strangest sensation I have ever had, being reduced to a pinpoint of light, only to expand my consciousness to then fill a vast universe of light. The point of light and the universe of light were the same thing. These tricks of size could only exist in an infinite medium. The part is the same as the whole. If you break off a piece of a hologram, the entire hologram is contained in the piece. Does each atom of existence contain the entire universe? Does the entire universe exist inside of its smallest particle? The mind cannot answer these questions. It is similar to the question of how many angels can fit on the head of a pin. The answer is all of them and none of them! But in these deeper states, the mind isn't active, the experience of knowing kicks in, and in this case, I know that the exquisite point of light, and the vast, infinite state of light were one and the same; not similar, but identical.

There was a knowing/sensing by the purity, the love, the quality and the magnitude of the experience, that Christ had responded. I felt something I would call "sacred compassion" as a pervasive quality, as though everything and everyone is held in that kind of holy esteem. I felt love beyond any earthly love I had ever experienced, as though everything and everyone is loved deeply. The light was a sacred light that was not different from grace. I felt as though I myself was this knowing, holy light. It seemed so complete. When I had for a moment become the whole of the inner world of that point of light, I fulfilled something that I didn't even know I needed to fulfill. I was shown that it is ultimately Grace, as a holy state, when beckoned, that draws us near. The purity and goodness of this state felt Christ-like.

In Sharyn's NDE she said she was drawn closer and closer to the light. She was ready to merge with the light but felt a barrier and was told she needed to return. As clinically alive seekers, our part is to refine our focus on the inner light. Grace, when it responds, seems to do the rest. I sought, meditated on and showed fascination for inner light and that night it eventually drew me in by its gravity. It pulled me entirely in and revealed to me its nature as a universe of light, the light of consciousness itself. Its benevolence was also similar to what Sharyn described in her NDE. This incredible benevolence was the living aspect of its own state of consciousness that signaled its conscious intelligence and its existence as pure, exquisite mind and heart combined.

I realized in a month long course on the 36 steps of creation as expounded by the great eastern philosophy, Kashmir Shaivism, that our minds are not really our minds. There is only one huge universal mind and our minds and lives are but voluntary limitations or disguises it takes. We are masks it creates out of the fabric of its own being and then wears in a brief dance, only to remove at the proper time to reveal itself to itself. This definitely mirrored the experience in this night of meditation. One might never be sure that he has experienced the ultimate, but I know from this experience that vast light IS, and I AM THAT. Is there more to my higher nature? I am sure there is, and I look forward to it revealing itself. Of course there is the even more daunting task of becoming established as a citizen of that world, not just a tourist. And as the masters say, the ultimate goal is living in that divine reality as our only reality.

An Honored Guest at Christ's Table

FOLLOWING MY LOVE OF the Christian story I once again chose a Christian holiday as a background for one of my quests for spiritual adventure. One Christmas, around 1975, I meditated for several hours in Yogananada's devotional style, again focusing on the third eye as I did that night in bed when I had the third eye breakthrough. I was feeling the Christmas spirit and my heart was warm and open. As I concentrated and relaxed, I moved deeper and deeper into the state of consciousness I was by now accepting as the natural progression of my meditations. My meditations seemed to have a particularly warm golden glow this particular Christmas season. I was at a rustic lodge called Asilimar on the edge of one of the most beautiful stretches of ocean in California in the Monterey Bay area. It was a personal holiday retreat. I had built a fire in the fireplace to bring the right atmosphere to bear upon the occasion. I made sure I had time to get lost in my inner world with no interuptions.

I was lying down to meditate, which seemed to allow me to relax into a deeper state of meditation. I was in a particularly joyful mood as I often am around Christmas. I incorporated the sounds of the fire into my meditation allowing myself to be warmed in body and in spirit. My mind went to holidays past and the good will they inevitably wove. I remembered the Easter meditation I had the year before. I relaxed into the moment as if a good spell was being cast upon me. I brought my mind back again and again to focus on the third eye area between the eyebrows and also on the feeling of warmth in my heart and the expansion happening everywhere in my inner space.

After 20 minutes or so of meditation, and as I continued to diffuse my concentration and allow the natural expansion of my state of consciousness to draw me into its embrace, I suddenly fell, like an unsuspecting guest leaning on a secret door in a hallway, into a brilliantly lighted inner room where a celebration was taking place (shades of the Easter meditation). I was startled, but knew instantly that I had entered a very special place. Then I turned and saw the long table, which seated all the guests at the celebration. It seated what seemed like 8-10 people, most of them on the two long sides. However, what was dawning upon me as my gaze went to the seat of honor was that it was Jesus Christ at the head of the table. It was a birthday party being held in his honor! Among those facing me across the narrow width of the table were some of the other Gurus in the SRF lineage, all of whom predated Paramahamsa Yogananda.

I felt such joy at being allowed to visit the room (inner space) of this celebratory state of consciousness that appeared to represent the state the SRF masters were in during that holiday. This was one of those times where I realize that I, like all other human beings, are worthy of being side by side with the great masters. I have had esteem issues along the way when it came to feeling honored by, let alone, equal or identical to God. Maybe some of you can relate!

In the meditation vision one of the spiritual masters whose face I could not see because his back was toward me, turned to face me. It was Paramahamsa Yogananda himself! He turned to me with such a beatific smile on his face that I began to bow at his feet to greet him and honor the radiance I saw in him. Before I could do so, however, he unloaded a couple of dozen red roses into my arms. He was welcoming me as a special guest of the Christmas celebration, honoring my spiritual essence and presence just as I was prepared to do with him. It was a mutual respect born out of a mutual love. It was love itself opening to itself as itself and for itself.

As the roses touched my arms, I imploded into a state of light and the room and figures disappeared. There was only the light. It was The Light all along, dancing in front of me in some of my favorite forms. I knew that this was some level of the state such masters live in and celebrate all of the time. They understand the truth of our oneness in spirit with each other. They know humility because as spirit, they ARE humility. Humility, as deep receptivity, is one of the natural and uncreated qualities of the divine. It is the universal Yin. Those enlightened ones create no separation because they know at their level of experience there is no separation between God and any of God's manifestation.

This experience, as much as any other, raised my spiritual esteem. In that meditation experience, I was about to bow. Instead, I was honored with flowers, and not by just anyone, but by the master to whom I was going to bow! It was a real feeling, a breakthrough in feeling worthy as a seeker, and planting the seed that we, and therefore I, may be equal in glory to God and the masters. As a Wyoming boy reared by a blue-collar family, it might take an extreme event like this to convince me of my spiritual worth! Nothing short of that would have given me the gut feeling of its truth.

I was drawn into the room of light and then drawn into a universe of light when I received the flowers. How is it that the universe draws us into itself, as if it has a gravity to it? I want to explore this next since it is a principle that predictably manifests itself in my meditations as well as the reports of many of the NDErs, including Sharyn.

The Draw Towards Growth and Enlightenment

IN MY INNER LIFE of meditation, I experience the universal light as having the power to draw me into it. In short, it is as if it has its own gravity. It is also true, that as a spiritual counselor, I have always felt that there was a natural draw towards spiritual growth that I have experienced in myself and have seen in the dynamics of my clients. Something in us challenges us to growth mentally, emotionally and spiritually. Perhaps what we call God is always drawing us into a merge with the highest and purest form of its own essence. This might create a natural urge to let go of self defeating habits, fears, anxieties, depressive thoughts and actions, thoughts and feelings of inadequacy, negative self images as well as obsessive, compulsive and addictive behaviors. We may be naturally drawn, by the wholeness of God, to let go of anything blocking our identity with that whole state of light.

Many clients over the years expressed disappointment that their marriage was not primarily need fulfilling. The dynamics I often saw at play was how their relationship was challenging to and stimulating of their own personal growth. Having them ask why the universe has brought them, in particular, together usually revealed a bigger picture. This overview of their relationship often included the "right-action" in their union that helped them accept a higher purpose for their pairing and helped them grow and expand from it. If the universe is constantly helping us remember WE ARE THAT, it would simultaneously be defeating, moment to moment, all limited notions we might have of ourselves.

I have experienced that the higher states have a draw on my awareness towards merging with them at higher and higher levels of consciousness as I repeat the experiment of focused meditation. There are several naturally occurring phenomenon that seem like good metaphors for the draw I experienced from the Self (the divine within). The first is the way a black hole in space behaves. When a huge star burns itself up and collapses into its own gravity, it creates such a powerful black hole in space that anything near it is either sucked into it and destroyed, or is certainly influenced by its pull. Yet a black hole cannot be observed itself; only the effects it has on other things are observable. Physical, observable light itself is bent from its straight path by the enormous draw of a black hole. In my experience, the effects of the Self are similar to the black hole's. The Self seems to have a similar draw and yet it too cannot be seen, at least by ordinary sight.

Think, too, about this; the Sun in our solar system has enough gravity to keep all of our wonderful planets predictably circling around it and yet it is only made of fiery gas. Why couldn't the power of our inner spiritual light have the gravity, like both the black hole and the sun, to draw us into its state, which is also experienced as the center of our inner universe? As I have shared before, Sharyn, and many other NDErs report being drawn up a tunnel and/or drawn into brilliant light. Each time I have sat for meditation, after I reached what I would call critical mass in my concentration, when a certain inner focus is achieved, the illumined inner space intensifies and begins to have a draw of its own. Its draw is toward merging my conscious awareness into its vast pool of light, at least to the extent I can surrender to that experience.

If God, being a dynamic whole, constantly draws our awareness into its state of wholeness, into a balance of its play of opposites, we would feel compelled to release our hold on body contractions caused by attachment and aversion that bind us to our onesidedness. Relaxing our hold on the knotted and contracted areas of our physical and subtle bodies, that keeps them in our own disfigured, conflicted, onesided shape, will challenge us to lighten the tension of our grip on these self defeating identities. Eventually we can follow the advice of AA teachings such as, "Let go and let God". Were we to relax our contractions little by little and focus constantly on our object of meditation, then the inner state of awareness could return to its natural full shape of perfectly balanced light. We could then feel whole and realize we <u>are</u> whole.

What are some of the more limited identities we find cloaking who we really are? One knot of our psyche/body might represent the notion that we are inadequate to life; we might think and feel that about ourself and may also act that out in our life. Another might be our addiction to angry defensive reactions and moods, both of which sour our relationship with others and also bring down the quality of our own life experiences. Some may see themselves as loving martyrs, ultimate saintly victims of life. Victim-hood is bound to be one of our sub-identities until we realize our identity with the Self, the creator of all things and scenarios. All of these are some of the attachments and aversions to life that keep us small. The different facets of our egos pull the round whole of consciousness into a jagged edged shape that is the identity we then consider our identity. There is a wide range of ego states and sub-identities that go from fairly benign, but limiting, to the absolute dysfunction of mental and emotional chaos.

Some people hold onto being right all of the time. Some hold onto their victim-hood. Some hold on to escape and avoidance through drugs, alcohol and other forms of impulsive, acting out behaviors. Some hold on to passivity and dependency, trying to force life to take care of them with no action on their part. Some build and hold onto material success at any cost. We do choose what I call playgrounds within which to play, and become attached to them. This attachment shapes our soul. All of the above can then counter the growth impulse to give in to our wholeness. All of our knotted, gnarly and naughty aspects, our unhealthy patterns and our dirty little secrets are just God's daily soap opera; benign play. We need no shame or embarrassment regarding them, but on the other hand, why wouldn't we want to rise above them into the world of light?

Paramahamsa Yogananda relates the story about communicating with a visitation of his own master, Sri Yukteshwar, after his master's death. His master tells Yogananda that he is working in more subtle dimensions with souls of people who have died with attainment of a certain degree of wholeness, but whose lives are so pleasant that they are content not to pursue the final state of enlightenment (mergence with wholeness, the supreme witness). His job is now to inspire them in the heavenly realms to become the divine witness itself and move beyond whatever level of pleasant wholeness they have achieved.

So, we must, while still embodied, let go, focus on awareness itself and allow the draw towards the light to pull us into the highest states we are capable of experiencing. Who would think that it is even more difficult to pursue the highest states when life gets so good from grace! I know about wealthy people who are unhappy with life, because a motivation for growth has not been honed by struggles. Likewise, many of those who have had to endure difficulties and setbacks, tackle their growth with zest and express satisfaction when their goals are achieved. No matter how good life is, or isn't, the divine witness is drawing us into a merge. If we release our attachments and aversions we are on our way to allowing the natural draw towards expansion and growth to take us all of the way there. Let Go, Let Go, Let Go; you won't really miss your attractions and aversions to all those limiting conditions! I promise! what replaces these "minor ecstasies" is so much more ecstatic!

The Entire Universe in Each Focus

WHY IS IT THAT whatever we are obsessed with and focusing upon seems to become so huge to us? We really are reluctant to let go of what has been sustaining us, no matter how meager it is in comparison to the Self. To me, this is a corollary of my experience of a point of light becoming the entire universe of light. Have you ever been in a meeting where two people begin to discuss something as inconsequential as a font for a sentence in a report, only to realize later that an hour meeting was totally taken up by that discussion, and everyone in the meeting made that topic of huge concern. Later, when consciousness has been normalized again, the meeting participants feel embarrassed to have made so much of such a small thing. Just like my focus on the pinpoint of light became the whole universe of light, whatever we focus upon becomes an entire universe to us and in factis the entire universe for us for that moment. This principle is why it is important to choose carefully that upon which we concentrate.

This has been an important principle for me to understand. It is one of the principles I see working behind the scene with obsession, addiction, attachments, and many other persistent deviations of awareness. Each moment of focus is the entire universal consciousness masquerading as whatever is being focused upon. If I am hurt, my hurt feels like a universe of hurt. If I am obsessed with Internet blogging, it may become my entire universe. If I am addicted to chocolate, then my entire universe during the day is about that. I am pulled into so many moments' focuses during the day, each having the gravity to capture me, and each of them becoming my entire universe at that moment. I give them universal importance and may want others to do the same. It is very important to know that everyone's awareness works the same way, and that it is one universal whole that we all feel and sense in each of its myriad forms upon which we concentrate. It is like the blind men and the elephant; we each are all absorbed in one aspect of the universe and believe we have discovered what it is like and intends. "The elephant is like a snake. No, it is like a tree. No, it is like a huge leaf. No, it is like a rope." The truth is that it is like all of these things and none of these things.

Anyone who used LSD in the 60's or 70's might remember that while using the substance, they were drawn into some inner idea or form and become completely absorbed by that. They might have seen the flesh of their hand disintegrate before their eyes and be certain that it is really happening. They are entirely consumed by that. But if they walk outside and smell the air, see the trees, or feel a breeze on their face, they are apt to fall into a rapture, which becomes their entire universe at that moment, the rotting hand being forgotten. The entire universe exists in an electron, or, in meditation, in a small point of light. And, a small point of light also exists as the universal whole. Remember, "As above (in higher inner states) so below (in our human lives)." What we experience in meditation reflects on how our life works. Our relationship to our inner universe has the potential to enlighten us about all of life, hence the importance of pursuing it. But our focus in the outer life brings the entire universal energy to it as well, sometimes inflating its importance in the moment.

Cesar Millan, the Dog Whisperer on an ongoing television series of the same name, takes obsessed dogs from their unbalanced family lives and places them with a dog pack that is balanced. In one show I happened to see, a dog was obsessed with chewing rocks. When his owner took him for walks, he would see a rock and have to chew on it, thus stopping the walk or the romp in the park. Cesar worked with him in a number of ways, such as making sure he was exercised, suggesting how to discipline him and teaching the owner to be the pack leader. However, placing the dog with Cesars balanced pack of 20 or so dogs balanced him out and helped him drop his obsession with chewing rocks. Membership in the pack normalized the dog because the other dogs provide corrections to deviant behavior.

I think nature has the potential for normalizing us humans. Getting back to basics and cooking out of doors, hiking, catching and cleaning fish, climbing, and sleeping with the sounds of nature surrounding you can shift your consciousness into a more balanced focus. Being near the ocean or staring into the night sky can also diffuse our intense addiction to the small (but universal sized) worlds of everyday life. No wonder vacationing is such a lucrative business and a necessity for all of us. We all need to shift our consciousness into creation in all of its wonderful manifestations, in order to loosen the pull of the sometimes irritating, sometimes frustrating, too often driven worlds we create, especially in urban areas, where getting to work by a certain time justifies driving over the speed limit and yelling at other drivers.

A point in the Whole, is the Whole, hence, be careful of what you wish for (focus upon) because you are more than likely to get it! Another way of saying this is, "Whatever your life is, like it or not, it is probably a result of one of your points of focus in the past and present." Think about this. How might this be true in your life?

To get a more balanced perspective and to make corrections for yourself, be sure to meditate, whether it is on nature or inwardly on the freedom of the inner Self. The larger picture can blend the elements of our lives together into a harmonious whole, making us less obsessive and placing them in better perspective.

A related principle is that focus can be in the form of either attraction or aversion. We sometimes say "I didn't ask for that, so why is it in my life?" However, in addition to "Do I secretly desire that?", we must also ask, "Am I secretly adverse to that, worried constantly about that, constantly defended against that?" Think of the example of someone fiercely independent, and aversive to the idea of dependency, who ends up with a disease or accident that renders him helpless and totally dependent. He is defending against (and hence equally or more focused upon) some kind of dependence, which he finally attracts to himself in the only form possible. Since he won't accept it consciously as a trait, he is leaving it to the unconscious to produce it and in my example, in the form of being ill and bed ridden.

Now, this is a simplification of illness. We know that genetic karma, life habits, stress and many other variables set us up for illness, but the point I am making about what we focus upon, through attraction and aversion, is also true and plays among all of the other variables mentioned. Perhaps someone averse to dependence who has a strong immune system, would not manifest dependency through illness, but through accident, or hearing loss. If our focus inwardly can draw to us universal light in abundance, what else can that same focus draw to us that will then threaten to devour us to varying extents, as we see most prominently now with drug addiction.

The principle of attraction through concentration (attraction and aversion) has been known and taught for a long time. However, it is not as often used in the inner world to attract different, higher states of consciousness. If there is a meaning for me in writing this book, it is in elucidating some of what I know is possible to attract inside of us, with enough motivation, focus and persistence. What inner delights can draw us near, if we are dying to see the light!

The Light Draws Me Near

A MEMORABLE EXAMPLE OF the universal pull of the whole towards higher states occurred for me at a meditation retreat held in the foothills of the Sierras around Truckee, California. This experience seems close to what some NDErs have experienced. It was a wonderful summer day in the early 1970's. My first meditation instructor, the aikido instructor, scheduled a weekend of meditation for us students at a ski cabin near Truckee California. The retreat site drew me into the joy of positive childhood memories of Wyoming streams, hills and pines. Some of the most edenic scenes of my childhood had all of the elements that were present in this mountain retreat: Summer sun shining through tall trees, the snap of dried twigs underfoot, the smell of pine needles, a slightly cooling gentle breeze, stumps upon which to sit taking in the dry warmth of a forest summer, paths into the trees winding up near rock formations just waiting to be climbed, and especially, the log cabin with its plank floors and sapling stair rails and hitching posts. I felt free the moment I stepped out of the car. Inside myself, I ran around jumping and tumbling, much like Sharyn did in her NDE, while my outer body moved around exploring the trails near the cabin. What a wonderful place for a meditation retreat.

We formed an 18-person meditation circle three times a day for a couple of hours each time. Some of the basic centering exercises that my instructor had us practice during our meditations in his home he would repeat over and over again at the retreat. Others he had us try were more experimental, intended to demonstrate to us a particular divine portal he was emphasizing at a particular time, through which to establish ourselves in the pure awareness of some particular aspect of spirit. The meditation exercise that laid the groundwork for my most intense experience in that retreat was a combination of both a typical grounding exercise and a unique approach to a universal center of light.

We were guided as a group to ground ourselves and melt into an already existing pool of light. After about a half hour of this kind of suggestion, my teacher had us shift our meditation to a vertical column of light that he also suggested already existed within us as the subtle spinal column in our energy body. This was not entirely new. His teaching always included the idea that we were already one with our spiritual body and just needed to settle into it. The part of the meditation technique that I dreamed up that day to help me travel up that column of light was to imagine being on an open elevator which itself performed all of the effort of the meditation, making it effortless for me, and took me ever upward through each level of light to the top of the spiritual ride, to the penthouse of light at the top. I envisioned this, from my Eastern Spiritual knowledge, as as traveling through each chakra, or energy center in the body, up to the most transcendent energy center at the top of the head, the Sahasrara.

There was something special about this particular retreat, but the idea of letting the divine elevator do all of the work was a technique that stilled my mind like no other had to date. Being intuitive, imaginative and visual in my perceptual mode, the idea of a divine ride in an open elevator up a column of ever-finer light was the perfect tourist's journey on a vacation tour of inner space. I became more and more absorbed in the experience. Illumination of a finer and finer quality of light filled my inner space. I began to identify more and more with the brightening state of light which at first was ground, or context, and was now becoming the foreground of my experience. I was merging with the expansive backdrop of life, a universal state of light and sound. The sound seemed to be a subtle vibration of a glorious, conscious electromagnetic field.

I didn't hear a heavenly choir, but the states of consciousness I visited that day reminded me of that feeling. Later in my life I touched upon these ethereal feelings listening to Gregorian chants and subsequently listening to Russian orthodox chants in churches in Moscow during a training I helped deliver there in the 90's. However, in the retreat lodge that day there was no music playing in this meditation exercise. There was only the feeling connected with it as I relaxed into the ride into the light of the upper realms.

The process of my journey into light was the usual blend of self-effort and grace. Along with a strong intuitive function, I inherited a very quick and busy mind. I have noticed over the years that many people who are labeled ADHD (Attention Deficit Hyperactivity Disorder) also seem to have strong intuitive functions that they are often distracted by, though I am aware that twin studies suggest that if one twin has ADHD, there is a 75% chance the other one will too, which shows the strong influence of genetics. For the quick minded intuitive, it can be distracting to see and imagine all of the possibilities in a situation. I am often moving quickly from one concern or issue or unfinished piece of business to another, imagining solutions, role playing conversations in my mind, noting my impressions and reactions, and rehearsing solutions.

The entire process of this meditation consisted of guiding my mind back again and again to the exercise. I would go off on some tangent such as wondering if I was following instructions and pleasing my instructor to then having some imaginary confrontation with him where I was convincing him that his opinion didn't matter, to then imagining he asked me, and no one else, to help him lead the group, to then drawing my mind back to the open elevator slowly ascending the column of light, to when we were going to have lunch to …. Well, you get the picture. I repeated this process literally hundreds of time in the 2 hours we were participating in this meditation exercise, though the mental content changed each time around. The more self-effort I made to focus my mind on the practice, the more luminescent and expanded became the state of consciousness within and around me. I was literally ascending into a higher, brighter state of being. The exercise was so aligned with the real structure of inner consciousness that most people in the group later shared that they too experienced the brightening of their inner state as they ascended.

After an hour of the guided meditation, suddenly the shaft of light spontaneously morphed into a scene of the sun shining a huge colomn of heavenly light through semi translucent clouds. There was a shaft up through the clouds filled with an ever-brightening light as one looked further up into it. It was very like the religious scenes depicted wherein God or angels are floating high in a break in the clouds while a heavenly light shines down through the clouds and illumines some praying soul who is enraptured with God's grace. You have all seen this picture somewhere, sometime. As primitive and simple as that scene can seem, with the sun-through-clouds representing God's-light-through-heavenly-clouds, my journey upward was nonetheless like that.

I was feeling humbled, blessed, glorified, sanctified, radiant, luminescent, holy, full of God's countenance as well as many other religious and spiritual feelings, when all of a sudden I was spontaneously drawn or sucked up from the elevator and through the tunnel of light in the clouds, emerging just above them in a scene which I at first did not understand, and then which reduced me to tears.

I was drawn through the clouds into a place of brilliant light above the clouds where a group of dozens of white robed beings were clapping, swaying and celebrating pure spirit. They also seemed to be celebrating my arrival to their state of being! When I realized they were rejoicing my success at achieving entrance to that particular state of divine light, I was filled with tears; they were tears of humility, surrender and acceptance in response to their unconditional love and celebration. I was being honored and the mutual love was so strong and the moment was so sacred that it defies words. I was overcome with profound emotion.

I know that the sacred specialness I experienced has to do with the glory of God's consciousness, not any specialness of mine, though I also experience that consciousness to be me, my higher nature. Ultimately I can say that it is the glory of my own true nature.

What I knew in an instant in this rarified transpersonal realm was that the radiant beings swaying, clapping and celebrating my arrival into their sphere represented a soul group of which I had been a member before this lifetime and of which I am still a member. I felt like the prodigal son who had come home after his wanderings on planet Earth. It was like the reunion of a monk with his fellow monks after years of travel around the world. I was the center of their attention and they were the center of mine. We were together again, not on earth, but above the veil of clouds separating secular life from divine life. There was recognition of at least one level of my higher identity as a divine soul full of light, love and celebration. They were all that was holy, as was I.

My joyful tears began to bring me back into the room with all of the other meditators. My instructor's voice also brought me back into the room as he continued to guide us through the exercise. I was so moved that I needed to be alone. All of the people in the group respected this and no one asked about my tears or my experience. I walked into the trees still feeling holy and profoundly moved by what had happened.

At first the meditation practice had been filled with self-effort. I had to re-focus my mind time and time again to an elevator traveling upward into an inner light. Then, I felt as though I were being drawn up into a world of light hosting many glowing white robed angels without literal wings. This draw through a tunnel of clouds might be the most similar experience I have had in meditation to the NDE experience of being drawn up a tunnel into the light and encountering beings of light. I saw wingless robed angels - spiritual beings who were now disembodied, or whose higher identities gathered in a finer, lighter realm and knew something of the divine mystery.

I visited many states of consciousness in that weeklong retreat, but that one experience captured the most important aspect of my transformation from individual identification to spiritual identification; it helped me remember that life is worthy of celebration, and particularly my sincere efforts at spiritual discovery and growth. It was similar to Yogananda's gift of roses in the Christmas meditation that I mentioned earlier. I still have to remind myself whenever I forget that I am worthy, in the same way God or Universal Consciousness is worthy, and am the most holy of holies and the most sacred of sacreds. I am the pure light of God. as we each are!

The other truth I experienced is embodied in a saying that the master of my current spiritual path repeated to us over and over, with great sincerity: "If you take even one step towards God, he will take ten steps towards you; that is his nature." I experienced once again that if I use my effort to contact God through constant refocus on him/her as light, then that self effort will summon the light of grace which then draws me into it. Over time, if I focus with strong intent on the light at the end of the tunnel, I will be drawn into it by some mysterious magnetism it possesses and be invited to release any hold I may have on a more individual identity. In the end, I will be surrendering to my own subtle Self-hood, which, in the final act, consumes even my acts of surrender!

Universal consciousness, disguised as a human being, feels the pull toward its own light in inner space towards Self awareness and realization. As pure awareness, however, that same intelligence feels the pull toward artistic creation and manifestation of untold universes. To repeat what I introduced in an earlier chapter, creation, sustenance, dissolution, concealment and revealment represent the five-fold play of God, according to Kashmir Shaivism, a profound eastern philosophy. Light densifies to create and sustain and lightens up to realize who it is, then dissolves back into itself, only to begin to manifest as creation again. There is always this figure/ground play as the seesaw of manifestation, and, alternatively, of Self-realization teeters back and forth. All of this happens all at once, all of the time, eternally. Our minds can't grasp it, but at a deep soul level we can experience the truth of it. As the divine in disguise, we experience this same flow from creation to dissolution and back. We are flooded with creative possibilities at all times, manifest some of them (creation), keep them alive for awhile (sustain) and then see them disappear (dissolution) as things change. For some of this process we may be ego centered and think it is all due to us (concealment), but there are times, as we reflect on this process, that we realize it is the divine at work (revealment, or grace).

The Fountain of Infinite Possibilities

IN CONTEMPLATING THE RECURRING idea presented here that life is a play of consciousness, does it at times seem to you that your life has been one long challenging play? If so, those moments might have been enlightening moments. It is so difficult for us in our state of limited understanding to relate to the extremes in life. In this global, media-driven day and age, we shake our heads at war, genocide, spousal abuse, child abuse, torture, and the extremes of greed, disloyalty and other forms of people's inhumanity to people and nature. We have all felt guilty for having thoughts, ideas and fantasies sneak into our consciousness that would have us experience some perverse pleasure in life at a cost to another human being. I will always remember President Jimmy Carter's statement to the effect that he was guilty of having committed the sin of "lusting in his heart."

Over the years, we have been reminded by various religions that God is good and man is bad, first through original sin and then by all of the sin that follows from man's basic sinful nature (or from other lists of thou shalts and thou shalt nots connected to a particular religion). Even the system of Yoga, which does not see mankind as bad by nature, has yamas and niyamas, which are the equivalent of the Ten Commandments for Jews, Christians and others.

But no matter how you look at it, God has allowed so called sin to arise in creation. God could have created a world devoid of bad behavior, but didn't. What is God's relationship to so called sin? If we attribute all good to God, and see him granting free will to us, then it appears that humankind has blown it by creating a warring, unfair world.

However, the experiences shared in this book suggest life appears real but is only a play. God (our "God-Self"), in my experience, is apparently not bothered by all of the things that upset us so much. If one were to accept that we can merge with God and realize we are one with God, then it is God who plays both roles of good and bad, sacred and evil, and it remains for us to merely discover this truth and align with our higher nature. It would appear that we are created out of love, and there is no original sin.

In the deepest of meditations and NDE's, God is experienced as the ever-flowing, blissful fountain of infinite possibilities. Kenneth Ring's chapters that discuss the live review process in his latest book, *Lessons from the Light,* shows again and again that there is nothing God isn't and can't accept. The fluid state of love behind the life review is unconditional.

The deeper background of spirit present in everything in creation is experienced to be alive, conscious and intelligent, shaping the evolution of each object of creation over years or eons. This fountain of cosmic ideas flows in the background at the center of each human being, and we have evolved as a species to the point of being able to awaken spiritually to the god force within and experience its creative essence. As the primal artist, God's flowing fountain of infinite possibilities is the flow of creative thought that is destined to become life in all of its splendor and all of its degradation. It is God's idea, and no other, that becomes our delight and our most horrific reality. But, if creation is nothing but the materialization of God's creative thinking, then how can we accept or experience God's mirth at the worst of it?

The truth, though it must be tested by each one of us in our meditations, is that what we humans experience as a reality is really a play. Shakespeare speaks of this (Life is but a stage…). We enjoy our own attraction to virtual realities such as movies, T.V., video games, and internet productions, not realizing that God, as the Light of Consciousness, is munching popcorn and watching, in 3D IMAX in his/her own infinitely huge multiplex, all of the movies we call life, meanwhile, spewing forth a fountain of alternative realities constantly. God is the ultimate theatergoer (theater creator too), however, Supreme Intelligence has an infinite number of eyes and sees all movies on all theater screens simultaneously. This intelligence is also the scriptwriter, the stage, the stage crew, the actors and the audience. The reason the term enlightenment is used for our moments of clear vision is that we see, in that moment, the truth of life as a delightful play of our own higher nature. A truly enlightened being is never lulled into delusion, but is constantly in the bliss of the cosmic joke, enjoying the play of life, while experiencing it as only that.

If we add free will to our understanding, then we know that we are not different from God, and we too, as "THAT", are producer, scriptwriter, stage, stage crew, actors and audience to our own productions. As an ever-flowing fountain of infinite possibilities, I do, by conscious or unconscious intention, select the pool of possibilities I will swim in and either cavort around like a dolphin or drown in my miseries as a neglected, victimized outcast. The reason liberation feels so good is that we are liberated from the last level of our own victim-hood, believing we are at the effect of life, that we are a passive victim of life.

The Tarot card named "The Lovers" shows a devil holding the chains of a man and woman as if in captivity. However, the secret wisdom of the card is the looseness of the chain. At any time we can realize that since we are the creator, we can lift the chains of bondage from our souls and realize we have always been free to splash in the everlasting fountain of infinite possibilities, laughing at the nature of the divine play that we are. Of course, the waters are most loving, ecstatic, joyful and delightful in the higher realms of the light itself, with our favorite saints and teachers as our companions.

As I contemplate this fountain of possibilities, I find myself thinking as it. When I began to express myself as "THAT" for the next chapter of this work, it flowed like a spring of pure joy, and I realized it was a flow from my very own essence, my heart. I initially experienced some reluctance to so brazenly identify with the divine publicly. Yet this is based upon the oldest of truths. This is the teaching of many eastern philosophies of enlightenment taught here in America for decades. In America In the first half of the 20th century in Pennsalvania and other east coast locations there was an era of western and eastern spiritualists claiming the truth that we are one with God. The Christian Science church and other positive thinking movements grew out of this influx of spiritual teachers. Paramahamsa Yogananda himself came to America to teach at that time and taught this same truth.

No matter how many spiritual masters assert, and mean, "THOU ART THAT", it is still quite something to take ownership of it. However, writing as the Self, from its point of view, which I do next, became a real test for me of the depth of my understanding and acceptance of truth. I am always changed by the flow of truth through my heart and brain and hands to the page. Truth, as I write it, lifts me to its higher states while at the same time challenges my non-acceptance of it. I deeply hope that my effort in the next pages can produce a valuable process in you, the reader.

So Many Stories to Tell

As MYSELF, *supreme* Self, "Supreme Awareness", I have so many stories to tell. I am a constantly active creative mind. How many times have I created universes and how many universes have I become. Where do I begin a story that has no beginning, nor will ever end? Which of my infinite dramas do I like the most? Which repels me, which disgusts me? What if I love them all equally? What if they are all in their entirety only an expression of my love of sport and play; love of creating, love of nourishing, love of reclaiming into myself, love of getting lost in my worlds and love of rediscovering myself in my various worlds.

Have I confused myself already? But isn't my very existence confusing? As mankind, aren't I fighting wars over my existence, my nature, and which cast in my many religious plays I most favor? My nature is spiritual law but my nature is also free will and total unpredictability. No wonder I confuse myself. There is all past and all future in my present moment, yet at one level, the past came first and the future comes later. As you, I confuse myself with my voluntary limitations of identity and will. As you, I feel separate and lonely. I feel like a pea brain in a huge universe. I feel like I know little, but am fed inspiration and guidance by myself as I peer into my great beyond and into my endless labyrinth.

I am mystery only from my self-limited perspective, my mind peering through the human eyes I have become. By contrast, I am totally known to myself when my mind, as human, realizes that it is the "All-of-All", encapsulated in a dense vehicle for pure enjoyment's sake. Do I enjoy my dramas filled with torture, suffering and death? Do I enjoy them as much as I enjoy new birth, spring fields, and sunny moments on all of my beaches? Yes, in fact, I do. When, as the self-limited soul, I begin to understand I am blissful in every aspect of my creation, then and then only will I have followed my limited human intelligence to its source, my highest realms of being. Then and only then can I bust my cosmic gut laughing at my cosmic joke:

There is no such thing as a bad drama, a bad life, or a bad dream nor is there any such thing as a problem. When I, as the absolute, am acting as if I am a suffering human being with a problem, I am as delighted as when I am fully enlightened as a Christ, Buddha, Krishna or Mohammad. Even as a moral, caring human being who thinks that I will soon see God after I die, I am asleep, while as a soul celebrating my human plays of death and torture without moral reaction, as illusory dreams, I am awake. As the limited human being, it seems to me, that this is perverse, though this is my absolute truth. As Saint Francis of Assisi, I say that there is no such thing as bad weather, only different types of good weather. As he, I know the secret.

One of my secrets is that I am never in a hurry. In a timeless infinity, knowing as I do that reality is equal to infinity, I could care less that I dream I am a rock for millions of years before I am eroded away and become wholly (Holy) dust. Was I ever impatient about the time it took for that one little transformation? Never. Not a single second. I am not only patient, but I am patience itself. As I realize this in my human form, and truly accept this, then and only then do I truly relax and find peace. True peace is becoming patience itself; it is the patience to allow universal process to move at its own pace, and life with it, enjoying it all from the "Eternal Now". There is nowhere else to be, no one else to be, no other thing to be doing, no contraction over any thing, and knowing that it is all nothing, at least nothing but I, and as I, it is everything. Know you are I and I am thee and become free. Be patience.

As you, I may think I am being driven crazy. As you I am, but I do not take it personally. It is just that I am crazy, and as infinite mind, I reside in my human selves disguised as human mind, and as infinite/human mind, I entertain infinite possibilities. It all seems too much, nestled into an apparently finite space-suit of flesh, blood and bone. As I awaken to my higher energies as you, and become aware of my beyond-universal nature, though, I realize I have infinite space as a context for my infinite possibilities and fall into total peace with myself. What once appeared crazy makes infinite sense (cosmic pun intended). I am not crazy because I am you, I am crazy because I am I; but I am not crazy if you really get to know me (know you as me).

There is no story line like I pretend is true through my dramas as various religions. That is, I am not developing myself as mankind to a point where I take the good guys with me and send the bad guys to hell. How could I do that? I am the good and the bad, and none of it is either good or bad. As the pure, conscious witness, I have become whatever the infinite range of possibilities is that has played out through my material, biological, animal and human selves. I am the play of opposites, and, in fact, that is how I create. I become the tension between opposites as I move apart from myself to create. This is the true dynamism of my yin/yang, my Shakti/

Shiva or my Savitri/Brahma. The tension is so full of energy that it is a fertile field for creation. As I fall into the depths of the tension, I grow less aware of my full power and glory, and can prefer specific realms of my whole to others, further fragmenting myself into differing worlds and tribes. As the so-called "good guys", I hang out around groupings of some of my infinite possibilities, while as the so-called "bad guys", I hang out around other groupings of my infinite possibilities, but they are all my possibilities.

The dance of religions is just so many colorful flags dancing in the wind around the fact of my existence. But the flag is only an invitation. As each flag (religion) I offer so much love to my membership, along with community support and religious ritual and feeling. As each I proclaim one or another of my names and invite others to come partake of religious experience. If I, as a human being, notice one of my flags, then I might hear one of my own higher names and begin to remember who I am. But I try not to take any one flag too seriously, because a flag is only a flag, a colorful reminder, but not my whole truth. As religions, I have developed myself out of unenlightened human beings that I have become. If I follow the trail marked by a particular flag, I will eventually need to wander beyond the flag to find my true Self, my true being. As the saints and sages of many religions, I have transcended the religion to find my truth. I spawned a saying as part of my yoga dance that goes like this: The thorn of yoga is used to remove the thorn of worldliness from my side. Then, both thorns must be thrown away to know the truth of who I am.

There is nothing that I am not. I create all things, including all religions, out of the fabric of my own being. At my core (in my highest vibration) I am love, I am bliss, I am omnipresence and I am consciousness. I am pure, supreme awareness itself. How could any grouping of my infinite possibilities, all of which arise out of my blissful nature, be better than another? How many times as a minister or religious leader have I fallen into my dark side and do seemingly monstrous things? As he or she, I wasn't aware of my whole. In splitting my whole into different pieces, if I was only aware of my good and shunned my bad, I couldn't be aware of myself as whole until I also embraced the so called bad, because I am infinite possibility, both so-called good and so-called bad. Grace is full of infinite possibility, and still remains grace. I dance in joy to all of my infinite dramas. When I realize in my human disguise that I am both the good and the bad, I finally understand who I am. I am beyond joy. I am beyond suffering and pain. I am beyond delusion. Yet I have become all of those, so I cannot say I am not they and they are not I.

It sounds as if I don't care. In a sense it is true. As a mortal soul, when I finally realize that I don't care, only then can I find my true Self and exist in my enlightenment. I DO NOT REALLY CARE. By that I mean that I do not care how I use my infinite power and my infinite possibilities. That is the meaning of free will, which is part of my nature that I retain in my disguise as a human being.

As I limit myself to become creation and all things in creation, I can sense, through my human form, that I have free will to play in any playground I create. Do I care that I choose negative paths over positive paths? Not really. I don't care. Remember, I have infinite patience. If I knock the space suits off of a million souls over a million life times, I don't really care. It is just an illusory trick I play on myself. For myself as the individual soul, death is the equivalent of a terrifying and painful carnival ride. On the other side of it, as universal soul, I realize I am still alive and in a more free and flowing state, with the potential to merge and cease existing as separate from myself as the universal whole.

In my dance as most of the souls involved in negative lives, I have created my own circumstances in one life time or another that have led up to a painful life for me in this lifetime. For myself as souls that in a particular moment are not acting out a destiny, but are acting in free will, a painful life would represent a new adventure flowing from my choices and timing. The free will that I am and have taken with me to my limited human form allows me to freely explore any realm of my infinite possibilities for as long in that life as I wish. I do not care in the sense that I don't care how much of a mess I make in my human form because it is only drama; it is only a virtual reality. It is like the plays put on by small children for their own amusement and the amusement of their parents and siblings. Remember my role as Louisa May Alcott and her sisters; as they I was acting out my own divine process, entertaining myself and myself as others.

Do I, as a human parent really care that I, as their child, have made a mess with finger paints? So-called evil is no more than that to me. As soul, I am energy, and as energy I am never created nor destroyed, only transmuted and transformed. I do not care how long it takes me to discover that my love of murder is one-sided. The other side is always there, teasing me with its existence, and inviting me to embrace it too. The shadow that murder casts is tender respect for life, and the shadow always makes itself known. I don't really care because I am infinite patience. I can take forever and ever to awaken and can play the villain in millions of life plays. I am patience. I don't care.

Are there consequences to my choices? Yes. When I spend time in my so called perverse realms and commit what the collective must define as heinous crimes against man and nature, then that becomes the only universe I know, and I attract all of the opposites within that virtual reality. One life time I kill and the next I am killed. One lifetime I step on people to gain power, and another I am the pawn in some one else's game. When I choose (unconsciously meander into) a particular world, I get to experience all of the aspects of that world.

The play of opposites is everywhere because they are I, and as opposites I exist in each realm of my whole, apart from myself as pure awareness, the absolute. I am the proverbial hologram. All of me is in each piece, and each piece is in all of me. It is also true that opposite realms are being drawn into my experience in each realm, because I am always whole. My time spent in perverse worlds draws to me the world of morality. My time in the world of morality draws to me worlds of apparent human suffering. It is only illusion that I am only whatever virtual life I create. I am always my highest and my lowest, as well as the state of pure, blissful formlessness beyond the play of my opposites. I am always whole and infinitely and indefinitely that way.

In my human form, why am I so fascinated with the seemingly real virtual realities, like television, movie and Internet realities, or stage and theater plays? Is it obvious by now? I am an artist. In other words, as omnipresent, conscious bliss, I create, sustain, and dissolve virtual realities composed of people and things. I hide from myself as these virtual realities, and within these virtual realities, and then through my human form, I eventually turn my awareness inward to my true inner (and outer) reality, draw the grace of my higher being, and finally merge back into myself, never really having changed at all. So that which apparently changed, really never changed at all, but enjoyed itself as a very populated virtual reality, with many stories to tell.

No wonder I pursue virtual realities in my human forms; I am nothing but a virtual reality as my human form. If I feel that it is my human story that is real and meaningful and find meaning in being a good person and not a bad one, then I am trapped in my virtual reality, believing in it and attaching myself to one or more of an infinite number of creative stories. In this fashion I have become the so-called do-gooder, who might repress his or her own shadowy impulses.

Do I ever enjoy being the bad guy? As Jack Palance or Jack Nicholson, I certainly do. As some of the world's most infamous tyrants, I might expect myself to say I certainly don't, but that wouldn't be true. As those tyrants, I was an even better actor because I stirred a global audience to the kind of hatred that supposedly only I as the bad guy was capable of expressing. One of the values of being everyone and everything I become, with the free will that I am, is that I awaken myself from my dreams by what I dream. If I shock myself enough as a truly cruel and murderous being, I may awaken to the opposite and find a path to peace. When I finally do awaken, I always delight in the waking awareness "Thank God it was only a dream!" (Row, row, row your boat gently down the stream. merrily, merrily, merrily, merrily, life is but a dream). I scare myself in my dramas, just for the fun of it.

As a human being who is not yet aware of my supreme identity, I identify with the victims of the world and want to put a stop to human suffering. I can spend lifetimes as that human being working selflessly to have peace and stop violence, not understanding that it is my eternal play (when has there never been violence on earth?). As the human, I see working for peace as a noble thing to do. And it is. As a spiritual master, I advise myself as disciple to do good deeds, transform primitive instincts, help others, think of only love and Joy, see the world as heaven, identify with the bliss of God and so on. Doesn't that mean that as the Master, I see the good and the bad and want myself as my devotee to be good?

The trick I have created here is that as the master I am not encouraging everyone to do these things so that we don't go to Hell. As the true master, I know that as you the human being, I am identified with my limited human form and am banging around as if I were that, when I could be identifying with my divine nature. That is, I can merge with my absolute God-Self and enjoy my creation, the free will, the dissolution, and the hide and seek of my supreme consciousness, only if I am detached from form and outcome. It is my attraction and aversion, as you, and my passion for attraction and aversion, that act as super-glue and connect me or lock me into my more dense virtual reality as creation and the drama of pain and suffering that is part of my virtual human package (pain, illness, death and loss).

Many of the movies I create in my role as the human being have themes of protagonists preferring to be flawed human beings rather than saintly, as if accepting my flaws as a human is coming to my senses and embracing reality. Characters I have become in virtual reality, such as James Bond, are as bad as the bad guys in order to get the bad guys and take their sweet romantic rewards after stopping evil. As movie goers, I applaud them and identify with them. However, a glimpse of my ultimate truth in meditation, prayer, reflection or contemplation, reveals another reality. I am the unflawed spirit itself behind the so called flawed human being. As those who have had near death experiences and died and then awakened to tell what the other side was like, I know I am totally free from mortal life on the other side, and often don't prefer to return, though I know it is not my time and I must. My experience as some of these NDErs and as the true spiritual master is "I am free, I am free!"

In expressing myself here, I think I have said apparently conflicting things. On the one hand, I have said that I am an artist, with unlimited freedom to create. But I also have said that I am limited by my own five-fold, unchanging nature. How can I be both unlimited and limited? As God, I am unlimited in the number and types of virtual worlds I can create, sustain and dissolve. Any virtual reality can be created within me, and lived in, for a certain period of time. These realities seem very real to me in the form of the human beings I have become. But each one is just myself as my highest state of mind with a disguise of flesh and bone I hung on it. As the human soul, I think it is my own individual mind inside of me, but it is not. All mind is my higher mind. As God, I just surrender to the limited will, knowledge and power that goes along with the illusion of my being human, in a world of sticks, stones and bones.

So the unlimited creativity of my nature makes me say, as the human being, God is all-powerful and unlimited. However, as God, I am also limited by my very nature and my universal functions. It is the aspect of myself I know as unchanging, eternal, and predictably compassionate and forgiving. However, everything created is also deteriorating. As all of you, I eventually die. This is part of my fixed nature and function and is known in my human form as one of my divine laws.

There are corollaries of these laws too, such as what goes around comes around, also sometimes called the law of Karma, or in my physical universe, Newton's law that states for every action there is an equal and opposite reaction. Because my first act in awakening to my creative potential is awareness of tension of opposites, creation can happen. In my infinite mind as human psyche, this sets up the law of compensatory behavior. If I, as you, become too independent I invite into awareness the opposite, even if, as you, I must appear to become ill to express it (unconsciously) and then must be completely taken care of by myself as significant others or hospital nurses. If I, as you, have an inferiority complex, my dreams will compensate with images of being a King or Queen, or some other important person.

My unchanging divine laws point to the very nature of myself, and it is an unchanging nature, meaning I must surrender to it (i.e. will always forgive, always dispense grace, always sustain and dissolve what I create, and always lose and re-discover myself). To know, as God, my lawful nature is to know the unchanging grace that is always at my beck and call as the incarnated human soul. But to know my creativity is to know an unfathomable, unlimited artist with omnipotent power and infinite possibility to create illusory, temporary worlds.

As God, I must give myself, as you, what you want. As you I have created many movements that teach positive thinking. People come to understand they can have and become anything they can imagine and want. Though in their more popular forms, these are not complete philosophies or understandings of my full divine nature, they do, however, reflect a true part of my nature.

One of my limitations is that I must respond when called; I have no choice. What I, as the human, think about is really not human thought produced by a human mind, but is divine thought itself. So when I, as you, think of something, it is really my own mind, divine mind, thinking of that thing, and as God, I am bound by my divine law - what is focused upon or meditated upon becomes a reality and materializes; this is the way I create life.

In human form, this idea is appealing because it implies that we can have anything we want, and can have it again and again, with enough focus. There are corollaries that say we will get it more quickly and more surely if we also act as if we have it and then act in order to have it. But the point I am trying to make here is a little different. It is that as God I am bound to respond, and being bound is not having free will, so in this sense, I do not have free will. As God I am bound; and as God I have free will. Both are true.

Nothing I do as you can add to me, nor can anything I do as you subtract from me. I am here in my glory whether or not I as you pray to me. I am here in my glory whether or not I as you chant to me. I am here in my glory whether or not I as you meditate on me. But I as you may not realize this unless I as you do these things. I am here in all of my glory if I as you insult me. I am here in all of my glory if I as you commit horrific actions. I am here in all of my glory if I as you am secretly self-indulgent. But I as you may not realize this unless I as you stop such behavior. I am the Glory of Light and that can not be changed by action or inaction.

Thus ends my speaking in this chapter as Supreme Awareness, my higher identity. As the writer of this book, my purpose here is not to offend or confuse, but to provoke deep thought about who we are and what that means. If I am one with the God of all, then I must own and and realize that I love all I have created. And when, as the self-limited soul, I begin to understand that (that I love all of my humanness equally), then and only then will I have followed my limited human intelligence to its source, my very own Self. Then, and only then, will I realize the unconditional love I already am. Then and only then can I bust my cosmic gut laughing at my cosmic joke.

Our Love of Virtual Reality

WRITING THE LAST CHAPTER was a flow of bliss and joy. It felt good to be writing as truth and it felt like infinite wisdom was speaking through my writing. One aspect that resonates deeply within me is seeing life itself as a virtual reality. Every parent, and many who are not, at some time asks the question, "Why do we as human beings all spend so much time involved with external virtual realities like the computer, television and movie worlds?" In fact, in one of the "Out of the Mouth of Babes" emails I received, I read that a child once asked his Dad, "Daddy, are we live or on tape." Now there is a young philosopher in the making!

Our technology has been driven along a path to virtual reality in a way inconceivable years back. It is true that we do many good things with our technology. However, the uses of it that have most captured our imagination are for personal entertainment and human contact, such as television, movies, computer applications, video games, the Internet, Twitter, Facebook, phone/text messaging, chat rooms and so many others. Literally millions of people right now have virtual lives that are larger, and consume more time, apart from work, than their so-called "real" lives. The average adult watches up to 4 hours of television a day and the average child even more. People are drawn to the Internet for many reasons, including challenging game scenarios, interaction with virtual stores, virtual libraries, and chatting with "virtual" people. Others can even participate in various forms of virtual sex.

Along side of the technologically based virtual realities we live in, many live in the virtual worlds of drugs and alcohol . Whether street drugs such as marijuana, ecstasy, LSD, crystal meth, cocaine, heroin or prescription drugs that can be found in most homes, the reality-altering nature of drugs create yet another virtual reality in which to lose ourselves. I am not being critical of people for their attraction to virtual realities of various sorts. As it will soon become clear, I am convinced that one of the huge truths of our existence on the planet is that we are all attracted to virtual realities for spiritual reasons. This insight dawned on me one afternoon when we were barbecuing on the deck and talking to friends around our deck table about virtual realities in the form of drug altered states to which so many people

are attracted and addicted. It occurred to me that the altered states produced by drugs and alcohol, just like our absorption into all of these virtual
realms, might be a distortion of a deep thirst for the divine. It was not a
new idea that drugs and alcohol can mimic altered states that in some small
ways are similar to higher states of consciousness; as a spiritual counselor I
had made that connection years before. But seeing other virtual realities
too as a mimicking of the divine play became very clear to me as I sat there
on the deck that evening.

We were sitting with friends around a table on the patio deck that evening. The topic of conversation shifted to "zoning out in front of the tube".
I think we were also including the attraction so many feel towards the
Internet, particularly kids. Our friends had strong feelings about not
allowing their children much time to get all caught up in any of these "virtual" mediums. I actually have a lot of empathy for that point of view,
though I watch a fair amount of television myself. I do think we get too
caught up in those virtual realities, hence the admonition we get from
others to "Get a life"!

But these particular friends were displaying a lot of passion about the
draw of television and the Internet and how these mediums would consume their children's attention and would keep them from life activities.
The response that welled up inside of me surprised me as much as them; I
said intensely, "but life itself is only a virtual reality that we are all caught
up in." It was a real conversation stopper. No one wanted to go there. They
reacted as though I injected religious beliefs into a fun evening. They didn't
know what to do with my statement. They changed the subject and I let it
go. Inside of myself, though, I continued to think about it.

All of our arts, too, are virtual realities we create in which to get lost. We
consider them entertaining. However, less known and less popular are
some of the oldest teachings and scriptures, which assert, with confidence
born out of deep experience, that our worldly reality is actually just God's
entertainment. The difference between God and us (though the conclu-
sions in this book point to their being no difference) is that God, as God,
never loses His/Her identity in all He/She creates. God as us, however,
allows its own vast consciousness to act as if it is lost in its own creation.

Our attraction to virtual realities such as drug states, the new electronic
mediums, new romance and the like, is our attraction to being taken over
by various altered states of consciousness. They invite our mind to be suspended there; where "there" is the headiness of a high, or the journey
through emotions of a movie, or the instant connection with others

through a medium like the Internet. These virtual realities are cousins of the creative play of the divine.

If we accept that God, as Universal Consciousness, is an artist at heart, producing virtual realities out of its own conscious substance, then why wouldn't we be interested in the virtual realities that, on a smaller scale, are the result of this original creative impulse acting through us? Many people, particularly after Timothy Leary and Richard Alpert (Ram Das) shined so much attention on the substance, have used the drug LSD, expressly so they can be introduced to its virtual realities. We seek these experiences out perhaps because they mimic the divine play, and, in fact, recreate aspects of it, just as our lives themselves do. Our deepest nature is all about creating scenarios.

Some movie special effects, such as those in the old terminator movies, include beings made of energy who morph in and out of human form. They give the audience the feeling of changing from matter to energy and back. The new wave of vampire and werewolf movies relies upon this morphing effect for their success. These too are virtual realities that people of varying ages seem to love to traverse, again and again, as if morphing and changing form are aspects of our own reality that we sense are our own potentials.

Einstein's discovery of $E=MC^2$ demonstrated to all of us in dramatic form that the reality locked into the smallest particle of matter is such a phenomenal energy that we can practically become God ourselves in unleashing its power; at least we become the dissolving aspect of God, which transforms matter back into pure energy. Again, there is the idea of morphing from a more solid state to a more energetic one.

My realization at the patio table was that our attraction to virtual realities is nothing but a fascination with the creative process that creates something out of "nothing", and "nothing" back out of something. We are drawn to the God process in whatever form it takes, getting caught up in all of the virtual plays, whether as small virtual segments of non-ordinary consciousness, or life itself as a larger form of the same thing. We love altering our states.

We worry about our children getting too caught up in these many states, but maybe the important ability to teach our children is how not to be too caught up in any aspect of life, including these states, since it is all virtual. For the true seeker, this involves learning to love the play of all aspects of life as God's own divine entertainment. This is a tall order, but achievable.

Our free will can always be applied to making life a more and more loving, and therefore more enjoyable, play of divine consciousness. Souls, however, who choose to create and play in more painful and shadowy realms will no doubt always be with us in our "Eternal Now". Spiritual mastery implies mastery of all realms and energies of life. This is the call of our wholeness about which Carl Jung, and later, Joseph Campbell made us so aware. Can we learn to sport with pain and tragedy, lighten it up, heal its wounding effects, but accept it when it wins for the moment and transports loved ones into other realms of existence? Can we view it through transformed eyes, from higher states of our own being, and see it as God's sport? Can we be drawn up into the light to live in rarefied states and higher dimensions of Universal Reality, while playing our role in all of the dramas our life unfolds for us? Can we be "in the world, but not of it"? This is the challenge of all virtual realities, including life itself.

The gravity of the higher states of this inner light of ours is activated by concentration or focus upon them. Our higher states draw us out of our addictive concentration on the various virtual realities, including the subtly virtual world of life itself, into that which transcends all of those plays and dramas and is the witness of them all, Supreme Awareness itself, our highest identity. This is the mysterious relationship between self-effort and grace. As human souls, we make an effort to be aware of the pull towards growth from within. If we consciously respond with a step towards it, this puts us closer to the already existing attention our God-Self has on us, giving us the impression that it is activating grace, at which time we are drawn more strongly inward and upward into the brilliance of pure awareness, pure Spirit, pure Being. We take one step towards our God-Self (hearing its constant call) and it takes ten steps towards us, drawing us into its intelligent luminosity. But do most of us continue to hold on tightly to our limited virtual worlds? For most of us, the answer is yes, we do!

Sharyn's NDE gave her the rare experience of the Light of Consciousness that, by its fundamental nature as unconditional love, instantly freed her from her attachment to her life on this side. In the next chapter she shares with us the changes that resulted from her realization that life on planet side is not the only life that exists. Let's hear from her personally about this and some other effects her NDE had upon her and her life on this side of existence after her experience. Here is the love of my life, Sharyn.

Sharyn Writes about her NDE

As Ron's WIFE FOR almost thirty years, I have been a bit dazzled by his meditation experiences. It's almost like he experiences these states on a multi-dimensional level; he loses the sharp edges of his being into another physical state and then he feels the impact on such a deep emotional level. By now, you the reader, are aware of the spiritual realms he enters with a receptive heart and no expectations. He has always been very open about his experiences and I think very courageous in writing this book. The journey he is on is one that he embarks on with intent, with discipline, and with years of commitment. My journey has been a different one. I was not looking for a life-changing event and I have always been very private about my experience. Private not because I have ever doubted the reality of my NDE nor because I didn't think it might prove helpful to another, but because it is so sacred to me that it felt like it needed to be protected.

People always ask me, "Did your near death experience change your life?" That's so hard to answer since I don't know what direction my life - or my belief systems for that matter - would have taken if I had not had an NDE. I will say, "Yes - my accident certainly resulted in a life-interrupt." I was headed in one direction - New York to attend acting school in the Fall of 1959 - but because of my injuries and a follow-up surgery, my goals and dreams of going to New York were aborted. That change was obvious. Not so obvious were the subtle changes that were taking place within me. I was not even aware of what was transpiring until much later in my life and I still learn more about its impact as my life goes on. Have you ever held a Kaleidoscope to your eye, slowly turning it, watching the small slivers of color re-arrange themselves into a beautiful pattern? Each change is so subtle and so minute, hardly noticeable - yet when combined, present an altogether different and intriguing pattern. So it was with me.

Instead of the stage, I practice my craft in a therapy office as a Marriage and Family Therapist. My NDE experience has been at the foundation of my work and certainly colors everything I do. I feel grounded in what I know is true and curious about what I'm learning from others who have had similar experiences. It doesn't matter to me whether anyone believes me or whether they question the validity of my NDE. Questioning leads to exploration and anyone who knows me knows how much I encourage questioning; questioning is at the heart of my work. You don't have to believe in NDE's or altered states of consciousness, or separation from the body, in order to experience it - it is a truth and possibility beyond belief. The earth was round and rotating on it's axis even when we believed it was flat - the truth is beyond belief.

I was fortunate when I had my NDE experience. At sixteen, I had never heard or read anything about near death experiences. After all, this was 1959 and before the release of Raymond Moody's book, but I was fortunate to have a doctor who listened, questioned and believed. I was in the hospital for close to three months and Dr. Nichols would visit me most evenings at the conclusion of his rounds. The hospital was very quiet at that time of night - the bustle of visiting hours was over and the only sound was the soft padding of the nurses shoes as they made routine room checks. The lights were dimmed and I can remember how much I looked forward to having my doctor come in, look over my chart and then sit in a chair near the foot of my bed. He would stretch out his long legs and always ask for a report about how my day was. And we would talk. And he would listen. I finally decided to tell him about this rather amazing experience I had had and he really listened. He told me that another patient of his had a similar experience and he was very interested in what it all meant. He had a lot of questions and clearly would leave thinking about what I had shared with him because the following night he would have more questions. I am still so grateful to him. As an adult, I haven't needed validation of my experience and what I know to be true; however, I think I did need it as a sixteen year old.

How has it affected me? I know certain things to be true.

Number one: We all have a purpose in this lifetime. This has greatly influenced by work as a therapist. It has helped me not to get pulled into the "sturm and drang", the drama, of a client's life, but rather to look for the themes or challenges that are being presented to them. I always ask them, "What is this situation, crisis, transformation or relationship asking of you right now?" The answer is key to that individual's purpose. There is a perfection in the answer and a perfection in what is being evoked. As an inspirational message that Maria Shriver has on the wall in her office says, "The two most important days in your life are the day you were born and the day you find out why."

There is also always a higher purpose and I believe we are given opportunity after opportunity to recognize and fulfill this purpose. This is where the true joy and happiness lies. Life without a sense of purpose is what harbors deep feelings of emptiness, bitterness and sadness. We all know that mentally and emotionally, there often is a void deep within that leaves us feeling without purpose in our lives, and I believe this is a deeply spiritual issue. I know from my NDE that I have a purpose in my life that certainly was not fulfilled or even known when I was just 16 years old. Of course, I have my own personal issues to resolve and grow from, as we all do, but I also know I have a greater purpose. I was told that I had a specific purpose, that purpose had not been actualized, and I would not be allowed to stay on the other side until I had served that purpose. My purpose? Within a year of my accident, in my Freshman year at University of the Pacific (UOP) in Stockton, California, I was introduced to a Ralph Waldo Emerson quote which I have carried around ever since.

"To laugh often and love much; to win the respect of intelligent persons and the affection of children; to earn the approbation of honest citizens and endure the betrayal of false friends; to appreciate beauty; to find the best in others; to give of one's self; to leave the world a bit better whether by a healthy child, a garden patch or a redeemed social condition; to have played and laughed with enthusiasm and sung with exultation; to know even one life has breathed easier because you have lived... this is to have succeeded."

Number two: There is a time for crossing over to the other side and it doesn't necessarily make earthly sense. To all of us left behind, it is always too soon to say good-bye to our loved ones, but spiritually it is never too soon for those leaving us. I have yet to hear from anyone who has had an NDE that they wanted to hold on to this earthly lifetime; what I have heard and experienced was a longing to continue, or return, to the other side. I felt such a deep recognition of a state of being that was complete in itself that I did not want to return to my regular life. My identity of "Sharyn", as an individual, disappeared into "I am who I am but not limited by my Sharyn-ness". Words still limit me. How can I be myself but not be limited by my self? How can I be an individual but have no boundaries and be part of something far greater? How can I be conscious of both at the same time?

What I contemplated long and hard during those many nights in the hospital was how could I not want to be separated for a day from my life and my friends, my crushes, my social life and yet be willing to let go, to detach, to another whole level of existence with no regret or no sense of longing. That just didn't make sense to my adolescent mind. It took many years to finally find the answer. The answer? I had returned home to my true state of being. I remember a phrase from my early Sunday School days which finally made sense to me, "Spirit is the real and eternal, matter is the unreal and temporal." [*Science & Health with Key to the Scriptures*, by Mary Baker Eddy].

Number three: There is a Higher Power, an all pervasive consciousness - a God. It doesn't matter what name we use, there is something bigger than we are who is all-knowing. There is a divine play that is occurring and we are all connected to it; we are all part of it and it has nothing to do with whether we believe it, accept it, rally against it or don't care anything about it. There is no decision to make regarding whether we want to play - we are all players. Back to my theater roots, "All the world's a stage and the men and women merely players." Ah, Shakespeare...

We are given all we need to succeed in whatever role we are playing this lifetime and the results are up to us. A second poem introduced to me at UOP struck me at a very deep level and it was probably the first poem I ever memorized. The poem was by Rudyard Kipling and at the time I didn't understand why I was so drawn to it. However, I did know it was important to always keep the book close at hand so I could refer to the poem. The poem was written in 1892 and opens with:

> *"When Earth's last picture is painted and the tubes are twisted and dried,*
> *When the oldest colours have faded, and the youngest critic has died,*
> *We shall rest, and, faith, we shall need it - lie down for an aeon or two,*
> *Till the Master of All Good Workmen shall put us to work anew."*

People always say to me, "So you're no longer afraid of death, right?" That's not quite true. I think about death a lot - probably more than most people. I'm not afraid of the process of dying because I do know it is a transition and that the transition can be a different journey for each of us - the dying transition is just as individual as our living has been. I know that this part of life is an unknown chapter in our lives and that it is not an ending but is simply a continuation. My reluctance to embrace death is because I have come to really love my life on this side of the curtain. I am not in a hurry to let it go and say good-bye to the people whom I love and who have enriched my life. I have been blessed to experience not only the unconditional all pervasive love on the other side of this existence but also the deep love that this lifetime has given me for my husband, my children, my niece, and my extended family here on earth. I'm one lucky lady.

PART II - Meditation Exercises

MEDITATION EXERCISES
ON VARIOUS
PORTALS OF LIGHT

Near Death: A Necessary but not Sufficient Condition

IT IS WELL KNOWN that many people are afraid of death (not so much among NDErs and STErs). Death is quite a teacher, as evidenced by those who have clinically died and returned to reveal a lot to us about the nature of the Divine. Generalizing this further, I wonder if the brief death, illness, or other catalyst required for an NDE might not also present a natural basic condition for a perfect meditation; a still body. The cessation of observable motion in the body (stillness) might create a necessary, but not sufficient, condition for higher experience.

NDEs show us that with the body/brain stilled, we are drawn into ecstatic states of light, communion with divine beings, and especially, some degree of merging with the light and becoming one with God as the "Light of Consciousness" itself. In the yoga literature, one of the classical standards, *The Yoga Sutras*, by Patanjali, teaches meditators that to experience the (divine) Self, we must "Still the vrittis (modifications, thoughts, energy waves) of the mind." Patanjali compared these vrittis to ripples on an otherwise still pond. Patanjali likens the still mind to a mirror surface on a pond, when there is no breeze or other agitation rippling the water. With the surface still, we can see deep into the pond, which would represent seeing more deeply into our Self.

Patanjali spends a great deal of the book cataloguing all of the various modifications of which the human mind is capable. We must still the tendency to think about existing objects. We must then curb the tendency for dwelling on myriads of inner images. There are even our abilities to join images and/or create images. There are so many tendencies in the mind that the average person can't imagine stilling them all and resigns himself to the carnival ride of his mind.

However, when a person clinically dies, in his NDE, the body/brain has become completely stilled because the body is dead! What better atmosphere for a still mind can you find than a still (dead) body? If this is true, then this condition fits Patanjali's suggested practices like Tapas (austerities to purify the body), Asanas (practices that still the body) and Pranayama (breathing exercises that still and energize the body and mind). To experience the Self, we must first still the body/brain, which helps the mind follow, just like the pool of water must still before we can see deeply into it or see what it reflects.

Many techniques for meditation, in fact, are to help us still the body and mind. The physical form of Yoga, Hatha Yoga, aims at stretching and relaxing the body to calm it and bring it to the "here and now" of our awareness. It has deeper aims too, to balance the flow of prana in two nerve systems that intertwine up the subtle body's spinal system, which creates the right conditions for awakening the Kundalini energy, the dormant spiritual energy at the base of the subtle spine. In this chapter, though, I am focusing more on the effect yoga has to still the body and mind. An ending pose in many Hatha Yoga routines, the "Corpse" pose, simulates <u>being</u> a dead body in order to obtain perfect relaxation of the body/brain/mind system.

At the level of physics, the body is an energy system made up of electrons and other particles madly swirling about their nuclei. There is an interesting chapter in the book *Forbidden History* named "The Physicist as Mystic". To the spiritually awakened, the body's energy is not dead and inert, but made up of living, aware intelligence. With the addition of this notion, a spiritual master accepts all of the findings of Nuclear Physics. And even some Physicists, like Fritzjof Capra, accept the idea that the energy that has become matter is in fact Divine Intelligence. A German philosopher, Friedrich Schelling once said:

> "*God sleeps in the Minerals,*
> *Dreams in the Plants,*
> *Thinks in the Animals,*
> *And Awakens in Man.*"

Einstein originally discovered that the amount of energy tied up in matter is expressed by $E=MC^2$ (later modified due to his discovery that the universe was expanding). If you multiply the mass of an object times the speed of light squared (a huge number), you get the amount of energy that will be released when that mass turns completely back into energy. We know this from the atomic bomb. However, if you add to the equation something that reflects that E (energy) represents <u>intelligent</u> energy, let's say the letter "I", this gives us an equation more reflective of what enlightened beings might experience (hence their enthusiasm and focus): $IE=IMIC^2$. This would translate to Intelligent Energy equals Intelligent mass multiplied by the intelligent speed of light squared. My only point here is that higher states of conscious have the power referred to in the formula but are also conscious.

The creative aspect of the whole, of her own free will, and with the delight of an artist, assumes limitations to become everything in creation. The cosmic joke for me is that behind and within each and every aspect of creation shines the bliss-face of the divine being. In a cartoon I have developed in my mind, a scientist looks at the smallest particles (waves) through whatever miscroscope is needed and sees that particle smiling back! I remember hearing Alan Watts say in a presentation, that he smiled to himself one time when he saw a gas station attendant pumping gas and acting as if he was not God.

Mantra repetition, counting breaths, staring at a spot on the wall, concentrating on a hymn or chant, focusing on the heart space or the "Third Eye", settling into one's center, sensing a subtle energy body and so on and so on are all ways of stilling the body and mind through focus. Just as stilling the body stills the brain and mind, so does stilling the mind automatically still and relax the body because it is the modifications of the mind that excite the body and vica versa. There is a story I heard but can't reference about someone who doubted the power of the mind as a tool to enlightenment through spiritual practices. A spiritual master chided him at a meeting and suggested he was a fool and had poor understanding. After being humiliated by the Master in public for a number of minutes, the somewhat intellectual and egoistic individual finally exploded at the Master. The master quickly said, "See the power of the mind? It took only a few carefully chosen words for me to cause your mind to totally transform the state of your emotions and body. If your mind can do this in a few minutes, why do you doubt its ability, over time, to take you to God?"

It seems to me that most meditation practices do, in fact, in their own way, simulate this aspect of the NDE. If there is one divine process, with its laws and nature, and if NDErs tap into or are drawn into that process when temporarily dead, why not make a conscious effort to imitate the basics of these NDEs as a path to deep connection and eventual merging with our divine "Inner Self". My own meditation experiences have added understanding of that divine process, as well, and can help frame the important aspects of the meditative process. As you might expect, this doesn't necessarily suggest radically new approaches to meditation, but might underscore many of the practices already known that are based on the truth of the divine process. And as I have pointed out before, the stories and experiences of the NDErs and some meditators are truly inspirational and can motivate us all to continue to focus on The Light, to prime the pump, until it must, eventually, draw us into its ocean of consciousness.

Dying to See the Light

FOR MY PURPOSES HERE I want to discuss NDEs, the experiences that are actually punctuated with a brief clinical death. STErs may have had catalysts that cause the body and mind to become still enough to also experience transcendent states, but I want to use the idea of brief death as a platform for building a meditation exercise that imitates as much as possible that aspect of Near Death Experience.

Dr. Alexander spoke at Sofia University recently about his NDE that he recounts in his book *Proof of Heaven*. His dramatic experience lasted 5 or 6 days while he was comatose. He visited realms of conscious light so powerful and intense and loving that in his experience, they make our daily life seem small in comparison. One of the things he repeated more than once was that the brain and the little voice connected to its functioning are actually in the way of merging with the "Core" of higher consciousness. The fact that his brain was, in his words, like "lobster bisque" meant that that little voice was stilled completely and his higher sensing was able to travel to immense realms of conscious light and feel at one with them. This is the sense that I have in mind of clinical death being a great stilling of the mind that allows an experience of higher states to unfold.

By now you might wonder how the death experience can be incorporated into ones's meditation practice. A word or two might need to be said to differentiate what I will propose here from the growth techniques of the 60's and 70's, where the goal was to visit our own funeral, visualize ourselves dead, see the mourners at our funeral, be a mourner at our own funeral and allow ourselves to react to our own passing. I performed that exercise with many groups in those two decades and found it extremely profound and helpful in assisting a person to find their love for themselves, work out unfinished business with respect to friends and relatives and with respect to how they were living their lives, see how much or little they meant to others at the mock funeral, and discover what they wished they had done differently, which they now could include in their ongoing lives, since it was an imaginary death.

The technique I will suggest here is different from all of this. It is more like playing dead. Remember the old westerns where the good guy apparently got shot and was lying there dead while the villain celebrated and thumped his chest? The good guy would then abruptly sit up (white hat still on) and point his pistol at the villain, who had by now holstered his fire arm, and capture the bad guy once and for all, leading him to jail on his horse with a lasso pinning his arms to his sides. The use of the dead body experience of the NDE as a meditation technique would be more like this, insofar as we are playing dead, but not to experience our own death. In the meditation technique, it would be to release our mind to roam the land of light.

Since some people might not be able to easily get beyond the idea of being dead. An image that I want to suggest instead of your own death, that still might capture the essential quality for this meditation, is the stillness of a person that is being so still that the butterfly they are watching a few feet away won't even sense they are there. A friend of mine felt this might get around using one's death as the meditative image. That kind of stillness, like the death experience of the NDEr, is a perfect condition for freeing the mind to roam in other spaces.

The title of the previous chapter was, "A necessary but not sufficient condition." I chose that phrase to say that while it is necessary for the body and brain to be stilled for one to experience an NDE, one's awareness might not always be focused upon The Light. The stilling of the body is only step one of the meditation process, just as it is in the NDE. The NDEr might find that their mind is in a tunnel, in a field or meadow, in space, in a dark space and sometimes even in a house or other building before it sees and travels towards the light.

The second step in a meditation that is based on the NDE is to take advantage of the stilled body to then focus in some way upon the light at the end of the tunnel, both metaphorically and literally speaking. In the experience of those witnessing their own NDE, there may or may not be a tunnel leading to it, but the light still appears and intensifies in their field of consciousness. Remember, the light is an intelligence, welcoming us with love into it's embrace. It is looking for us as we are looking for it. I want to first examine the technique that is suggested by traveling through a tunnel, since it is such a common experience of NDE'ers.

One of the most profound meditation experiences I have ever had was based loosely upon that very image, and was presented earlier in the book under the chapter title, "The Light Draws me Near." This breakthrough meditation I shared shifted from a meditation practice to an experience that had a life of its own, not controlled in any way by me. As I rose in the open elevator towards the light above, I broke through a tunnel in the clouds into a glorious light and a cloud rimmed with heavenly beings, welcoming me to their realm of existence in consciousness. I have repeated that technique with varying results since then, and have refined it to a process that maintains a centered platform for the experience, allowing one to practice the first step of being as still as in death, and yet also allowing the experience of traveling effortlessly towards the light.

The approach to this particular portal to The Light may not represent a new and untested meditation experience, but because it mimics the most common and powerful aspects of the NDE process, it can give reliable form and structure to many seekers' spiritual practices, and might add an element of believability and enthusiasm for the practice since the techniques themselves are the experiences of people who made the journey there and back.

Step #1 - Be as Still as a Lifeless Body

Preparation - Sit upright in a relaxed posture with loosely crossed legs or sit in a chair, perhaps not leaning back onto the backrest, but sitting forward on the edge of the chair with feet flat on the floor and back straight and elongated. If necessary, it is ok to lie down.

Meditation - Imagine yourself in a beautiful meadow, one you remember or one you create as you perform this exercise. See the beautiful flowers in the meadow. Now see a colorful butterfly landing on a flower near you. How still would you be if you did not want to be seen or heard, not even your breathing, by that butterfly. Allow time to relax and still yourself more and more as you sit or lie there taking in the beauty of that which you see.

- • ~ Sit upright with your backbone straightened, head resting effortlessly on your neck (lie down if necessary).
- • ~ Be comfortable and let your body relax into gravity. Let your breathing naturally slow as you settle into your own subtle awareness of being.
- • ~ As you become still, allow your body and mind to focus on that absolute stillness of the body. Settle into that stillness.
- • ~ Allow time for your breathing to become still. Your mind will become still because the seat of the mind, your body, has become still.
- • ~ Continue this exercise again and again for 10-20 minutes

- ~ Sometime later, as your mind/body unit is approximating the stillness of a butterfly watcher, allow the subtle-most awareness of your still mind/body to move freely within and around your body.

- ~ Sense that you are the pure awareness that is aware inside and aware outside, all around you.

- ~ Now allow yourself, as awareness, to move through the entire room. Allow yourself to be the air in the room, and allow the air to circulate throughout your still body.

- ~ Settle into still awareness of the room and your inner and outer body as if you were the state of Awareness Itself, alert to the expanded stillness that you are.

Step #2 - Stillness Travels to the Light

Now add to your state of awareness that your chair, or you, if floor sitting, are resting on an open elevator pad at ground level, much like the elevator platforms on stage that bring performers and their instruments from below stage to stage level.

- ~ Imagine the elevator, with you on it, is at the bottom of an upward tunnel, like a huge well-shaft.

- ~ Be sure your actual posture and the imagined posture on the platform are the same and upright (unless lying down), relaxed, and the body stilled as in being invisible to the butterfly.

- ~ Feel the elevator begin to slowly move upward toward illumination that fills the upper part of the well-shaft and beyond.

- ~ There is no efforting for you. You are being still so as not to be detected, but you are being elevated towards the light by the elevator, which is doing all of the work.

- ~ Allow the elevator to imperceptibly move upward. You are meditating while sitting on the elevator pad and it, with no effort from you, slowly moves effortllessly upward towards the light.

- ~ Your awareness is imperceptibly brightening as you inch towards the bright diffuse light above.

- ~ You are passive and receptive to these small changes of intensity of the light that are automatically produced by the elevator moving toward the light source.

- ~ Imagine melting little by little into the light that shines down into the tunnel, as if that light is an expanding electromagnetic state that, as

Supreme Awareness Itself, permeates through the sides of the tunnel, as well as your body.

- ~ Now let yourself be moved upward into brighter and brighter spaces of light and allow your entire awareness-of-being be drawn into them.
- ~ Your pure awareness, which is contained within and without the body, is aware of the full experience, as the entire awareness/mind/body unit is moved through the tunnel into the light.
- ~ Your awareness is expanding and merging with the increased brilliance encountered as you move out of the tunnel into more and more light, your body stilling more and more.
- ~ Beyond the tunnel is a more and more spacious and more and more light-filled space, as the still mind/body-centered awareness moves into that expanding space of light. There is all the time in the world to allow this to develop, since the elevator is barely moving upward.
- ~ Stay focused on your sense of the light, whether it is showing itself to you or not and let go again and again as if it is doing all the work of pulling you into its state.
- ~ Continue this way for 30-60 minutes, depending upon your willingness to continue to re-focus upon yourself as pure awareness, expanding and brightening effortlessly.

Rounding the mind up is like herding cats. Rounding up my mind is like herding ants! I have needed long meditations to give me time to travel a thousand mental pathways and return home again and again to my focus until I am allowing myself to settle into the process that is the heart of the meditation. Rather than chase cats or ants, the process of returning to our focus is like settling below all of the mental traffic and just letting it pass by. A fellow meditator in a spiritual book group to which I belong reminded me of the strategy of seeing the busy mind itself as spirit in the form of words. Rather than corraling them all, instead transcend them - the image of sitting under a bridge hearing the bubbling of a stream while the sounds of traffic (our thoughts) above on the bridge are allowed to fade into the background.

My most intense experiences came from hours and hours of straight meditation, though I don't recommend someone start with this strategy. Such powerful energies as we are invoking through concentration are not to be invoked in high doses before we have explored higher energies long enough to know our reactions to them and their effect upon us. The organization ACISTE, www.aciste.org [http://www.aciste.org/] , for which I am an adviser, is dedicated to helping those who have difficulty with any spiritually transforming experience they have had, including NDEs. It is not uncommon for indiivduals to have difficulties with the intensity of their spiritual experiences.

As I have mentioned before, my Jungian Analyst reminded me more than once that if I wanted to invite up into consciousness the unfinished business of my life, all I would have to do is begin meditating regularly. To this day, I am still not able to be completely regular about my practices because so much energy is awakened and my mind/body can still be reactive to it.

I do recommend, though, that the reader take a break from reading right now, and follow the above contemplation. One way to experience it would be to dictate it into one of your recording devices and play it back as you close your eyes and follow the suggestions of your own voice. Your job is focused sensing, your body's job is letting go to gravity, and the job of Grace is to transport you to other dimensions of light. Remember that meditation is the continual act of dropping below the chatter of the brain/mind while focusing on your divine nature!

Inviting a Shift

SHARYN INDICATED IN HER chapter that she was attached to peers, to acting as the star of her senior play and to her plans to study acting in New York. Yet in a moment, she experienced a shift into that divine consciousness that exists behind life as we know it. Like a reset button on some of our hi-tech devices, it reset her entire life in allignment with higher experience and higher purpose. As she just wrote, "I am one lucky lady." She also followed a path of giving and receiving love and in her own way meditates and falls into states of love and bliss; "Liquid Love", as we call it when we fall into it together. Her experience acted as a wake-up call to that higher realm of joy and light and she has moved toward that higher state in so many ways in her life.

It seems to me that there are meditation practices suggested by the portals that are forged for us by the NDE. The first one that comes to mind is the foreground/background shift. We can call this one "You die and then Shift happens!" (could make a good bumper sticker). As happened with Sharyn, our lives are spent in pursuit of dreams and aspirations, pleasurable life experiences, relationships and so on. Being also a human-animal, our lives orbit around territoriality, attraction, repulsion, and power over ourselves, others and the environment. Our first area of focus in life is all of this foreground stuff: external life itself. Of course, some people are more introverted in nature and more inwardly focused by nature. However, when people die for a short time and/or lose the foreground body experience (literally transcend their connection to the body and the physical plane), they experience the shift to states of splendor, light, and the radiance of nature.

A few experience other realms with relatively more darkness. For most, though, whether it is fields of flowers, open sky, various states of white light, or as Dr. Alexander mentions in *Proof of Heaven*, dark spaces of radiant light full of joy, one is shifted to freedom never before experienced and expansiveness that all the time was in the far background of the person's life. Most of these people open themselves to love that is like no love they have ever experienced in their life on earth and joy that is beyond belief. Roughly one out of five clinically revived patients report they experienced something like this, and the fact it happens at all demands our attention.

One of my first meditations was at Esalen Institute and occurred back in the late sixties. This happened before my experience of light in the psychic reading by Anne Armstrong. During a break in one of our week-long encounter sessions, one of the trainers in Will Schutz's "Flying Circus", Seymour Carter, introduced us to a simple Zen style meditation. He lined us up along a wall and had us pick a spot upon which to concentrate. We kept bringing our awareness to that spot over and over again while counting breaths. At first I was aware of the surface of the wall became like the ocean's surface with waves of dancing molecules. This might have been purely an ocular shift.

Whatever the cause of this part of the shift, I cooperated with it instead of fighting it, and solid Ron and solid wall began to morph into shimmering wall and shimmering Ron. I also found myself drawn from outer concentration to deep inner space. This part I am certain wasn't just ocular. In fact, I was so deep inside that I literally could not draw myself back out to speak for the rest of the afternoon. I was lost in the background state of "the peace of God, which passeth all understanding". I was in a deep state of awareness that was at peace with all that was going on around me. All of my usual foreground was just going on as usual and didn't even touch the background with which I was for the moment completely identified. I again felt in the world, but not of it. People would speak to me, and I would nod my head, but I was captivated by the peace I had dropped into and I could/ would not speak back. As the day wore on, I thought I would never come out. However, as I engaged in outer activities, the pull of this deep inner space lessened, and by evening I was back to normal discourse.

In looking at this experience later, I realized that I had never before given that inner space a chance to captivate my awareness. Once there, it felt like my tab-A had been properly inserted into my slot-A for the first time. It felt so natural and whole and right. In fact, it felt so right that I would do anything to get back to that inward home, where I could kick my shoes off and spend some serious down time. Something in me was saying that this space was the real space of life more-so than the outwardly directed life I had lived up to that point. Though it wasn't infused with light like future experiences, it drew me into a deep expanded state, opening a path to later light-filled moments.

As mentioned before it seems next to impossible to be aware of anything but the body and mind's restlessness in the first part of a meditation . You are telling your body and mind to settle and calm, and they seem to rebelliously do the opposite. You have sat down to meditate on the Self, and instead, your mind gets all involved in the tension in your legs, the irregularity of your breath, the soreness in your neck and shoulders, the flashing of the mind onto unfinished daily goals, self criticisms, longing and yearnings, and the combination of hunger pangs with thoughts about one's favorite foods. We also run into the paradox of practicing meditation; letting go, in order to produce results, has to be letting go of letting go, letting go of producing results. Try to figure that one out!

But even if the foreground at the beginning of our meditation is a stressed out body/mind/emotional chaos, still it is concentration on or awareness of this dynamism that can allow the background to eventually pop into the foreground. Let's assume, for example, that the meditation begins with an awareness that is focused on an initially stressed but slowly relaxing body and mind. If one herds one's awareness back enough times to this chosen foreground, then one has established the point of focus (body, emotions and mind). Automatically, through the tension that always exists between background and foreground, the background is challenged to appear.

As I mentioned earlier, the mechanism for this is the inherent wholeness of God as the Self. Universal Consciousness is an infinite, homeostatic force. That is to say, to focus on any one aspect of the whole is to automatically draw the rest of the whole into one's focus to join what has been singled out. It is understandable, then, that through the gateway of body/emotions/mind awareness the figure/ground shift can visit us as a shift to pure inner consciousness as a meditation progresses. While sensing the relaxing body, the calming mind, and the quieting of breathing, a tension builds up inside, leading to a shift to the background of light. As this newly awakened inner consciousness begins to become the foreground, the relaxing body and calming mind can, for at least a few moments in the beginning, become background. This shift is the first step to higher, subtler dimensions that form the background of existence.

Of course beyond the play of opposites exists an absolute reality, the primordial formless. Call it Satchidananda (the omnipresent, blissful light of consciousness). Call it pure spirit or the void. Whatever you call it, it is Supreme Awareness itself. That ultimate ability to experience and know something is itself the formless absolute. A quote attributed to St Francis of Assisi that I have always liked is "What you are looking for is what is looking." (Brown, R., *The Little Flowers of St Francis of Assisi*). When we eventually master holding both the background of inner consciousness and the foreground body/mind/world dynamism in our awareness at the same time, we realize that Supreme Awareness itself is the ultimate state, holding within itself the universal play of opposites, the play of light and shadow, the play of Yin and Yang that we call life. What would it be like to use the figure/ground dynamic as a focus for a meditation practice.

The suggestions below are simple ways to create a portal into higher experience. As such, they give the mind a focus to allow the background spirit to appear as foreground. As practices they are something to experiment with as often as possible. Like prayers, many trials may have to be performed to eventually draw a response. It is a long term approach that may or may not produce results right away. Spiritual practices are not for the impatient unless they are prepared to refocus again and again.

Inviting the Divine Shift (part 1)

- ~ Assume the sitting posture either in a chair or cross-legged on the floor. If in a chair, rest your feet directly on the floor or a wool blanket. If sitting on the floor, cross your legs loosely and place a cushion under your buttocks. Sit upright, but relaxed.
- ~ Take some deep breaths, hold them and then relax the body as you release them. Do this several times. As you feel the body relaxing, allow your breathing to slow down naturally.
- ~ Feel your comfortable body and breathing as a pleasant foreground experience.
- ~ Track your breathing and feel the body grow more and more still and relaxed.
- ~ As you relax into all of these pleasant foreground situations of relaxing body and slowing breaths, allow yourself to enjoy the sensations. There is nowhere else to be and nothing else to be doing.
- ~ Keep your concentration upon the warm comfortable body sensations and continue to let go into them.
- ~ While aware of the slowly breathing, relaxed body, ask how you can be even more relaxed and more still.
- ~ Allow the breathing to slow as if to not be heard or detected. Let go to a relaxed awareness of all you experience inside and outside of yourself.
- ~ Continue this relaxed focus for 15-20 minutes, always rounding up your focus and bringing it back to the pleasant body/breath situation, letting go of more and more tension and distraction.

- ~ Now, as you continue to renew and refocus awareness to the body and breath, begin to watch for any natural shift happening in the more subtle background of Awareness Itself.
- ~ After 30-40 meet the natural shift of consciousness to the light filled background with an expanded sense of brightening that you imagine is there. Imagination is the tool we use to try to interface with that background of conscious light that is omnipresent.

Be patient with this part of the process. I have observed that those with a more practical and less imaginative approach to life will probably feel changes at the kinesthetic level (more relaxed, more warm feeling in their body, other pleasant sensations), while more intuitive and imaginative types of people might feel swept away with currents of energy, with visual expansions and with more brightening of their inner/outer space. The intensification of background spirit is happening in both cases, but the mode of perception is different for sensate based personalities versus the intuitively based personalities. Be happy with whatever your mode is. Intuitive types usually need to develop their more grounded sensate functions and sensate types often need to develop their intuitive abilities. Meditation can help in both cases.

Inviting the Divine Shift (part 2)

For the remainder of the practice, keep both the relaxed body/mind in your subtle awareness, but also begin to include what might be in the background of your meditation. Part #1 of this meditation is like first meditating on the warmth you feel in your body and the sound of your breath. Part #2 is to include awareness of the space in the room or beyond, with the understanding that what we picture in our minds can manifest as a reality.

- ~ Keep the warm, relaxed body/breath state in your awareness and add an expanded sensing of the background state of pure awareness, expanding your awareness to include the room, the house, the sky and beyond.
- ~ Sense a brightening background state, as you remain focused upon the body/breath state. If this seems difficult or uncomfortable, continue Part #1 of this meditation for a longer period of time.
- ~ If you feel success in expanding your awareness, open your heart area to it, as though the expended background sense of light is dancing with

joy or flooding you with love. This "acting as if" is a powerful attempt to "dock" with the background of joyous light. If it succeeds, then there will be a point where the background comes alive, has a life of its own, and leads you into states of being that it wants you to experience.

- ~ Go back to Part #1 of this meditation as many times as you wish. However, after doing this, once again send out a feeler for a more brightened, expanded state, "as if" it is there waiting for you to "dock" with it.

Continue this meditation for 20-50 minutes, depending upon your comfort in sitting and focusing and re-focusing. Afterwards, you can lie down in the corpse position, palms up, hands just out from your sides, small pillow under your head and neck, and let gravity have its way with you, pulling the tension out of your body and allowing you to relax in stillness. Sometimes it is only this last exercise that a true "letting go" occurs and the dance of light is sensed within.

Remember that this and other approaches to the other portals below are practices to add to one's daily life. The devotion to such practices will eventually connect us to our higher energies. What is in the beginning faith that this is true will eventually become the direct experience that this is true. Always keep in mind that this has been proven in a case by case method by literally millions of souls over the centuries.

Meditate Upon the Sublime Within your NDE

ONE OF THE MOST obvious meditations that is suggested by the content of people's NDEs is meditation structured upon the highest, brightest, shiniest, most loving, most ecstatic, most sublime images in that person's NDE. When I read some people's accounts of their NDE, they say things like they remember it well but long to experience it again. As a veteran of somewhat consistent meditations over the years, I know with certainty that the light is just waiting for us to call it forth. The NDE, from this point of view, is like a peak meditation that ought to leave us wanting more and doing everything in our power to bring it to consciousness again and again, until we are living each moment in that taste of heaven the NDEr was granted.

For those who have not experienced an NDE or STE, the images presented by these heavenly travellers can be beginning points for them as well. The descriptions of the NDE or STE experiences can give hope to a seeker who has yet to experience them. These meditation instructions I will suggest are therefore for NDErs, STErs and all other seekers. They will ultimately work most certainly with STErs and NDErs whether you have imagination or not, because for you two groups, it is not conjuring up something fantastic that you haven't experienced before. Rather, you are remembering the details of what you already experienced, either traveling beyond your clinically dead body, or being transported to an altered state by other catalysts.

Because you were given that taste of the divine, in whatever way that it happened, getting back to it is through the path of memory, now, not imagination. This meditation might not be different from what you do all the time (reflect upon your NDE/STE), however, I will try to make it a more intensely focused meditation.

Meditation is like the theme of the movie *Field of Dreams*: "Build it and they will come". Prepare again and again for your true nature to shine forth and eventually it will! If Jesus, The Buddha, Muhammad, the Dali Lama, the Pope or Krishna were visiting your city from time to time, you might send an invitation each time for a visit to your home. Each time, you would

sweep your driveway, clean and trim your yard, clean your house and prepare food, flowers and a special seat.

This preparation is analogous to the practice of meditation. Even if none
of these great beings ever took you up on your invitation, you would still
enjoy the preparation and thinking about them. If, eventually, one of them
did visit your home, you would feel that your preparations set up conditions for that visit to take place. Likewise, if the meditation practice below
is performed on a regular basis, perhaps interspersed with other meditation
practices (to keep the mind interested), then these practices of meditation
will eventually bring results, either in the form of inner experiences and/or
the experience of synchronicities and "lubrication" of your outer life, with
all of the little improvements that grace can bring. Without self-effort to
invoke grace, we may or may not notice the inner guidance and grace that
is the background of our existence. Meditation practices are both an invitation for our higher nature to appear and a practice of awareness that aids us
in noticing it more and more.

If your NDE was not so sublime, or was more frightening than positive,
which happens to a much smaller number of NDErs, then there might not
be memories for you to build this meditation upon. In this case, one has to
find the right memory or image to use and it may have to come from experiences other than the NDE, such as a perfect feeling one had in a perfect
setting on vacation while watching a sunset or gazing at a fantastic view.
Most people have had special moments they can focus upon that represent
a bursting forth of divine magic in their everyday lives. Another source of
mages for this meditation might be putting together an image related to or
sparked by others' NDE images from the chapter *The Glory of the Light*.

Meditation on the Light of the NDE

- ~ Either sit on a chair with feet flat on the floor, or on the floor Itself,
  with legs loosely crossed.
- ~ Sit as far forward on your "sitting bones" as you can (as though you
  are thrusting your butt backwards), yet keep the spine straight.
- ~ Let gravity have its way with you, relaxing you around the body structure or form suggested above.
- ~ Fill your entire form with a deep in-breath and then, keeping the form
  in place, exhale slowly and allow your body to relax around that form.
  Repeat this a number of times, depending upon your need.

- ~ Keep your awareness focused upon the lungs as the breath fills them and then empties out of them. Focusing upon them keeps your awareness on the heart area of our more subtle states of being.

- ~ Allow yourself to reminisce about the most delightful and delicious aspects of it. Was it dancing in the light, dancing to joy, feeling a "peace that passeth understanding", feeling a profound love or bliss circulating through your heart space or something else beyond your daily experience.

- ~ Whatever the sublime was in your NDE, bring your mind to it again and again as if it is a living presence within you at all times (which, of course, it is).

- ~ As your mind wanders or your body protests the discipline, gently guide it back to the memory, whether a body memory or a visual memory, and once again allow yourself to delight in it, swim in it, tumble within it, surrender to it, soar in it, dance in it, or in some other way be captivated by it as you were in your NDE.

- ~ The more you relax into it, the more opportunity you are giving to it to shine forth in the here and now, in the present moment, as a state of consciousness that is your true, highest nature.

- ~ Remember that meditation is about repeating again and again the inner preparation for an inner state to shine forth through the portal you are approaching.

The seeker who has not had an NDE can find wonderful images of the light upon which to focus in the chapter The Glory of the Light. Follow the same instructions above. Bathing in these NDE images is literally bathing in God's light and act as a spiritual shower whether or not they are immediately brought into consciousness.

Wrapped in Love

AS I WAS PREPARING this chapter I had a dream that my Guru cradled me like a cat for 15 minutes in a public program in front of other devotees and infused me with a high state of consciousness that I still experienced when I awakened. What a loving confirmation for me of the portal to the light I call, "Wrapped in Love"!

"Wrapped in Love" is an approach to meditation suggested by the "Life Review" phase of NDEs that Kenneth Ring reported in *Lessons From the Light : What We Can Learn From the Near-Death Experience*. I was personally moved by the experiences of those who had gone through this aspect of the NDE. As they moved into the light, their lives flashed before them in some form, but not as in the presence of a critical parent, but as in the presence of a compassionate, knowing, forgiving, loving and accepting being of light. They felt loved for all of their experiences. They were able to accept who they were and how they had behaved. They felt the unconditional love of a higher state of consciousness and were moved, in many cases, to have compassion for themselves for their past actions.

Again and again, the people Kenneth Ring studied amazed him with their stories of unconditional acceptance in their NDE. As I read these stories and Dr. Ring's analysis of them, I was reminded of Sharyn's experience and my various experiences in meditation. What first comes to mind as an example of this is the acceptance and unconditional love Sharyn felt in her NDE when she tumbled in the loving space she first entered upon leaving her body. She said, "Oh! This is that state that people try all their lives to achieve. This is the moment of experience they want to touch, that moment of absolute peace and absolute joy. And I am feeling that this is 'it' - true happiness."

I was reminded, too, of the tremendous love and acceptance of Paramahamsa Yogananda when, in my meditation, he represented Christ and the SRF lineage in placing a bundle of roses in my arms, as if to say "You are honored by us just as we are by you." The state he initiated me into with his gesture was one of fantastic unconditional love. I was also reminded of the celebratory acceptance of the soul group in the clouds up into which I was drawn in my elevator meditation during the retreat with my Aikido instructor, and the accompanying unconditionally loving state of consciousness.

In the Prologue to her book *Dying To Be Me,* Anita Moorjani shares this unconditionally loving state that she experienced while in a coma at the end of a long road of battling cancer:

"I then had a sense of being encompassed by something that I can only describe as pure, unconditioal love, but even the word love doesn't do it justice. It was the deepest kind of caring, and I'd never experienced it before. It was beyond any physical form of mine, regardless of what I'd ever done. I didn't have to do anything or behave a certain way to deserve it. This love was for me, no matter what! I felt completely bathed and renewed in the energy, and it made me feel as though I belonged, as though I'd finally arrived after all those years of struggle, pain, anxiety and fear. I had finally come home."

Later in the book, she adds:

"So I found myself with nothing but compassion for all the criminals and terrorists in the world, as well as their victims. I understood in a way I never had before that for people to commit such acts, they must really be full of confusion, frustration, pain, and self-hatred. A self-actualized and happy individual would never carry out such deeds!"

Mevin Morse and Paul Perry in *Closer to the Light* use the term "wraps" in speaking about the light, saying "Those who experience the Light say that it is more than just light. There is substance to it that 'wraps' them in a warmth and caring that they have never before felt." Their depiction of the loving light wrapping the soul in warmth and caring underscores the meditation experiences of mine too that helped shape this chapter's title, "Wrapped in Love".

This all embracing, unconditionally loving aspect of higher reality is itself worthy of volumes of books, and volumes are indeed out there. Why shouldn't it, itself, become a portal to the divine? It is for me, which causes me to want to share it here as an exercise for others.

At times over the years, when I was feeling bruised by life, wasn't able to go to sleep right away, was worried about issues in my life, or was very depressed over events in my life, I developed a sleeping pose (and self-talk to go with it) that lulled me into self-acceptance and sleep. I laid on my right side and placed my right hand on the left side of my face and my left hand on the right side of my face. I am cradling my own face between my two hands, as a mother might cradle her child's face between her hands. I then act as if I am that loving God both Kenneth Ring and Anita Moorjani write about and I say to myself things like "I love you very much. Everything is perfect in my eyes and you are perfect in my eyes. You are nothing but love. My love is your love. We are loving beings and can experience only love. I love everything you do as a delightful play for me of my life." My insides would loosen up, my guarding reactions to stress would relax and my mind would calm down, because I knew what I was saying was the truth; I had experienced it before. I would eventually drop into a beautiful meditation state and fall asleep.

As a technique of meditation drawn from both from meditation and the NDE experience, this self-love can be expressed in many different ways, each leading into a meditative state. If extremely stressed, one could literally choose a meditation posture that allowed one's arms to be wrapped around oneself. Sometimes I haven't wanted to sit in the proper yogic posture all of the way through a meditation due to feeling of stress, exhaustion, achy body or whatever. I find, in that case, that if I sit back in a comfortable chair, leaning into a soft cushion, totally supported, or lie down to meditate, even in bed on a pillow, I can feel as if I am supported in the arms of that unconditional state of love.

By now, both from your own experience or from what I share in this book, you have an idea of the totally loving and blissful state our higher consciousness is in. It is liquid love. It is exquisite bliss. It is wrapping you in its arms and loving you like a divine mother. All is ok. You have done nothing wrong, ever, because whatever you have done was a divine play performed only for the enjoyment of your higher nature. Feel and accept that total love.

PORTALS TO DIVINE LOVE

What are some images based on this truth that might serve as a portal for you the reader upon which to meditate in order to experience unconditional love as an aspect of the divine? I will present several catagories of these. Pick one or two of them that feel natural for you. If none feel natural to you, pick one you feel you relate to better than the others. Read them enough times to keep one or more in mind as a meditation.

Comfortable Position as Portal

- ~ Sit in a comfortable, fully cushioned chair, curled up in some position that you can sustain for the better part of an hour with your spine as straight as you can get it.
- ~ Alternatively, lie down on a soft couch or bed and either lie on your back with a pillow under your head or assume the fetal position, curled on your side.
- ~ Use a comforter or throw to cover yourself so you feel the comforting warmth wrapped around youl.
- ~ Remember a time when you were at peace, being comforted by someone or comforting yourself. If it helps, hug yourself in some way, as I did falling asleep, and tell yourself that you are a spark of God, a ray of light, a loved child of god, or some other divine creature loved by God.
- ~ Feel that whatever physically comforts you represents God hugging you and pulling you into his/her bosom.
- ~ You are God's beloved and you are being loved as you sit or lie there.
- ~ If it feels comfortable, allow whatever love you feel to be your love and God's love combined: One feeling of love both you and God share. That feeling of love is God, and you are THAT.
- ~ Bring your mind to this imagery for as long as you can. 10 minutes? 20 minutes? 30 minutes? Longer?

Water Element as Portal

- ~ Sit in a warm bath.
- ~ Sense that the warmth caress of the water is the flow of grace.
- ~ You are being massaged by the water because you are worth it.
- ~ The water becomes God's energy, comforting you and warming you.
- ~ You can repeat some of the initial steps of the first exercise to help you feel divine love.
- ~ Bring your mind to this imagery for as long as you can. 10 minutes? 20 minutes? 30 minutes? Longer?

Comforting Human Contact as Portal

- ~ Imagine someone holding you in a comfortable position. - Relax your body so that loving state can hug your insides.

- ~ Accept the loving support this outer structure provides for your insides.
- ~ Sense that your body is living material, glowing radiant with spirit and embracing you with complete love.
- ~ Feel the love and comfort flow in from the other person or from your image of that happening.
- ~ You can repeat some of the initial steps of the first exercise to help you feel divine love.
- ~ Bring your mind to this imagery for as long as you can. 10 minutes? 20 minutes? 30 minutes? Longer?

Imagining Yourself As Divine Love, as a Portal

- ~ Sit or lie in a comfortable position so that you can feel yourself as a comfortable glow of warmth and love.
- ~ Focus on that glowing radiance that is your own electromagnetic field.
- ~ Sense that expanding or at least connected with the electromagnetic glow of the entire room
- ~ Sense that the vastness of loving spirit is everywhere at once; that the whole world and universe is a glowing force field of love.
- ~ Love everything at once, inclding your body and mind. If you sense your breathing, sense that it is the entire universe breathing in and breathing out.
- ~ Breathe in love and breathe out tension. Repeat this again and again.
- ~ Allow your heart to unwind. Let in pleasurable thoughts and feelings.
- ~ Smile at the vast, loving presence that enjoys who you really are.
- ~ Experience yourself as the cosmic joke that the entire universe is laughing with and at.
- ~ Smile at your silliness for worrying and carrying on as if you aren't constantly and totally loved by the divine being (you are).
- ~ Smile at your silliness for thinking, even for a moment, that you are anything other than the playful, blissful universe of spirit itself.
- ~ Feel like you have a divinely pleasurable secret that only you are aware of: that you are totally loved because you are totally love itself, vibrating radiantly throughout time, throughout the entire universe.
- ~ Burrow into this state of luxurious love and peace for as long as you can sustain and bear it!

If you don't feel you have much imagination, then stick to the warm bath, the warm bed, warm chair or warm mat and pillow and open yourself to the loving support of whatever is surrounding you. Let this be a healing experience because it is spirit that heals, the light of pure awareness that heals, so the more you soak up the radiance of what is hugging you, the closer to spirit you become. This will work because it is true. Our mind may be chopping us up with self-criticism and blame, but during that same time, spirit is loving us to death with absolutely no criticism for anything we do.

The NDE experience, as well as those experiences born out of deep meditation, supports this approach because it is the true reality of our higher nature. It is love absolute and it is always loving us in spite of ourselves. Find out for yourself if this isn't true.

Guiding Affirmations on the Path

FROM KNOWING OUR DIVINE nature, it is possible to generate guiding affirmations for ourselves. These affirmations are not developed to be held over our heads as goals of actualization, but are developed as a feedback tool that both confirms to us to what we have actualized in our spiritual practices and also what we are still realizing is true. These affirmations also can serve as guides to prioritize each day's spiritual focus.

This is the list of affirmations I have developed for myself and use lightly and joyfully in and out of meditation. I am happy if I am living up to an affirmation on the list, but it is also delightful if I am not and am still stuck in a particular area of my spiritual development (like discovering your cat unrolled a roll of toilet paper; you know you have to teach them not to, but you can't help but laugh at their folly).

I know that life, as a play of the divine, is delightful to our higher nature, but I still find myself loving (attached to) some plays more than others; I must be, because I keep the scripts running over and over, and it isn't always the higher plays to which I find myself attached!

I remember sending a question to my spiritual master back in the early 1970's. My question for him was "Why doesn't my life support my being with you on the East coast like others are able to do?" I was obviously living on the West coast of the U.S.A. and wanting to be with him. My master dictated a letter to one of my favorite swamis and instructed him to tell me "It is your love that is keeping you from being with me." The swami said my master had given me something tantamount to a Zen Koan. To my master, it was all love. My love of my family, my love of my work, my love of being in control or all of the above might have been some of the love(s) that were keeping me from being with him, yet he was telling me, in his wisdom, that it was all love. It wasn't my arrogance or my stupidity that kept me from being with him; it was my love.

The unconditional love demonstrated in the life review of NDErs shows that loving acceptance is always there at the higher level of our identity. All of our mental machinations to the contrary are just mind games that disguise the truth about our nature as love. With this in mind, what would "Guiding Affirmations" look like? Let me share with you the ones that reward me with joy or challenge me to realize them. As you read them, remember **who you really are** and you will see that these statements are true of **that** you. Use them in the spirit of affirming, again and again, your higher identity and let yourself be that higher identity speaking the affirmations.

Spiritual Affirmations

1. I awaken each morning to the awareness "I AM THAT".
2. I am constantly in meditation, being my highest state, the supreme witness.
3. I am established in the living light of witness consciousness in the eternal now.
4. I love my past, present and future life unconditionally.
5. When I say "I", I am aware that I mean "I, the divine Self,"
6. I love my adversaries with the same love with which I love my closest friends.
7. I build my life on love, I give love, I receive love, I merge with love, I am love.
8. I am aware that every interaction with every person is a delightfully loving and joyous event in the NOW, whether I and others are aware of it or not.
9. I see God in other people and myself each and every day.
10. I am naturally charitable, wanting the best for all.
11. I send love equally to the heroes, villains and victims of life's most horrific catastrophes, calamities and horrors.
12. I experience God's presence in my life daily in synchronicities, inspiration, joy and guidance.
13. I delight in chanting, prayer, inspired thought and spiritual visualization, affirming my true nature.
14. I remember again and again and again and again each and every day that I am Supreme Awareness itself.
15. I wear the shawl of unconditional love wrapped around me always.

To the extent you identify, or attempt to, with your highest nature, you will feel the joy, love and acceptance of these affirmations. They represent meditations unto themselves. Perhaps you will find one that most represents what you need to remember at a particular moment in time and will use it as a focus in your meditation that day. Perhaps, on the other hand, you will find that repeating the complete list as many times as needed will transport you into that state for which you long. You may also add to this list by contemplating other truths about your higher Self. Write or say, silently or aloud, "As Supreme Awareness... (you fill in the blank), and repeat them with the conviction "I AM THAT TOO." For example, "As Supreme Awareness, I am fully present in my timeless, eternal now."

I hold workshops on strengthening our identity with our higher nature. It is amazing what shifts can occur in our awareness with affirmations of who we are as our highest nature. To take a full day to focus on our higher nature is so evocative of spirit and so affirming of true identity, that it serves as an awakening for some, and a remembrance for others. "As Supreme Awareness...", is a tool that yields the truth because it is based on the truth: I AM THAT.

To the extent that we are uncomfortable affirming our higher identity, and most of us will be with some or all of the affirmations, we can learn where our spiritual work lies. We can confront those areas with the truth of the affirmation and then empathize with the parts of us still needing to hold on to lesser identities that have served us in good stead over the years as we navigated our original family and then adult life after that. As my master suggested to me above, it is all love. I would assert that even your anger and resistance to some of the affirmations is love attaching itself to certain apparently opposing ideas and feelings. We hold onto our limited notions to have an identity. But every step we take in the direction of recognizing our supreme identity will be discovered to be filled with joy. At that point, the more limited identification will be effortlessly released.

Meditate on Being Supreme Awareness

THIS IS A TRICKY chapter because it has subtle nuances that might bother some people on the spiritual path. Their concern might be warranted, too, unless I can convey just the right attitude intended in performing the practices mentioned. In the chapter entitled, *So Many Stories to Tell*, I spoke of the challenge of writing as Supreme Awareness itself; writing as if I were the highest state of consciousness sharing and affirming my awareness of myself. One of the pitfalls of that kind of practice would be to be inflated by that exercise and believe I was special, different or superior, acting as that supreme awareness. Another pitfall would be to feel I was desecrating something holy and sacred by acting worthy of role-playing it. To some it would seem a sin to speak as if one was, in fact, the holy of holies; it might seem a sin to speak as the Supreme Lord and to dare to act equal to that highest state of divine consciousness.

There are other pitfalls too. What if our knowledge of the divine is misguided to the extent that we might think that God wishes ill on us in some way as punishment for our sins? I think these are reasons we do not usually approach teaching identity with the divine through a book or a practice. Maybe it is something only the Sadguru (true guru) can do; only that being can properly supervise our path to self-awareness so that we discover, at the proper time and under their guidance, that we in fact are at one with the universe, one with supreme consciousness and therefore with all of creation.

So, why am I suggesting that we engage in such a practice and why am I devoting a chapter to it as an exercise to bring us closer to our true identity? I do not envision it as a beginner's practice. I am placing it among the last chapters because it carries the implicit warning "don't try this at home" (unless you feel a strong affinity with the possibility).

After years of traveling the path, I arrived at a stage where I had been taught, again and again, "Thou art that". I was experiencing it in meditation, but I felt I still needed a more intentional practice of it to bring home to my mind that it was the absolute truth and that it was <u>my</u> truth. I remember a day in the car driving home from the local meditation center. I found myself at that moment acting out of duality, where I, as a devotee, was asking the Guru to shed grace upon me. I knew this was not the truth I experienced most deeply, nor was it the truth most deeply taught in my path. I decided in the car to begin at that very moment what has been a practice ever since then. I began to speak as the highest reality itself. The ride home was exilliarating and full of bliss. After that, I began allowing myself, in my spiritual practices and private daily thoughts, to use only and exclusively the language of identity with the highest state of consciousness and to shift to doing that if I wasn't.

As an aside, as I was writing this chapter, I happened to host a meditation program and guided everyone into a short contemplation of themselves as the highest. I had read words Lord Krishna had said to Arjuna. As I myself began the contemplation with the rest of the group, I noticed I was gazing through the third eye area and caught myself wanting to see the form of Krishna there. Instantly, my inner state of light, in the form of Krishna, moved deep within me and simultaneously sent a telepathic message, "I am this state you are in and I am looking through your eyes, not at you!" A inward shift occurred that settled me even more into that higher state, as Krishna, and the third-eye gazing dropped away. It all happened so fast that I broke into quiet laughter at that whole play of consciousness. As I mentioned in an earlier chapter, St Francis is also credited with this idea, saying, "What you are looking for is what is looking."

Now back to my breakthrough in the car. After my revelation and resolution in the car, instead of praying for grace to change my situations or feelings, I would start with identifying myself as that highest state of grace and then comment on my situation and/or feelings. "As Supreme Awareness…," I would think or say aloud, "I have created, through this human body, a difficult challenge with which to entertain myself." I would not only force myself to look at the situation in this way, but to verbalize it too. Then, my mind would begin to hear and accept this true identification with God. It sure put an end to victim-hood!!! From that day forward, there was no victim and there obviously had never been a victim, nor would there ever again be a victim. What a release and what freedom flowed within, over and out of me (Which me? Of course, me as the higher Self). I felt liberated from my own self deception. I knew this was right, I felt my freedom, as the Self, in it, and I soared ever so high with it. With this practice, I initiated a great change in my life. In fact, if I had to choose a single purpose for writing this book, it would be to bring this truth and practice to the reader.

I might never know how much my success in this was due to the medi-tations where I experienced the truth of it, how much the success with it was the gurus' teaching of it over the years or how much the success of it stemmed from the exercise I chose to do starting in the car that day, to anchor it in my mind and psyche. I only know that it not only stuck, but also has become my only practice, in this sense: When I meditate, I medi-tate as the creator who bestows grace. When I chant, I identify myself as THAT making sounds that I love and am. When I repeat one of the man-tras I have been taught, I am THAT making sounds that I love and am. When I do anything, I am THAT engaging in one of my plays in my crea-tion and do it with love, joy and bliss. Whenever I feel the troubled water of churning emotions, I remember with great joy and a smile on my face I am THAT cruising through rough emotional waters I created. If I am caught by a mood or feeling, I may go under with it because it is so intense, but I immediately go to my one practice and think or say "As Supreme Aware-ness......" My life has not changed; I love my wife and our life together. I still love my adult children and all of our enjoyment and struggle. I still love my spiritual practices, alone and in my spiritual community, though my spiritual community has become the whole world and beyond. Nothing has changed, except my identity. "Who am I" now has only one answer.

So how do I share this, as I seem impelled to do, without seeming like a fool, a braggart or a lunatic? How can I share it so that my reader can actually benefit from it? I am not totally sure. Maybe it is enough to have shared my own process with you the reader so you can judge how to use the truth of it in your own spiritual progress. Paired with mantra and med-itation, it brings potency because it puts the mind in the right attitude to succeed in meditation and in life. Certainly, if you know this truth, have been taught it or are even fairly certain that it is a universal truth, then maybe I can give a few tips in implementing the practice of I AM THAT, or, "As Supreme Awareness, I...."

Expressing Yourself "AS" Supreme Awareness

The portal to a direct experience of Supreme Awareness in this case is role-playing being God. Can you approach that? If you have practiced the affirmations in a prior chapter here, you have begun this anyway. Are you ready to embrace an intensified version of this approach? If the answer is yes, then here are some suggestions for you.

- ~ Be by yourself with some time to devote to this spiritual practice.

- ~ Be where distractions are at a minimum.
- ~ Have writing materials within grasp.
- ~ Be comfortable. If possible, sit upright, at ease around your firm but relaxed spinal column.
- ~ Now, instead of talking <u>to</u> God, talk <u>as</u> God. If you can see that God is in fact supreme awareness, then use the phrase, "As Supreme Awareness..." and finish it with sentences about supreme awareness.
- ~ An example might be "As Supreme Awareness I am aware of everything, everywhere in each of my eternal nows." Then you might repeat "As Supreme Awareness, I continually experience love."
- ~ Keep starting sentences with "As Supreme Awareness..." and say what you think is true about your God-Self. If not much comes to mind, then go the the earlier chapter entitled "Guiding Affirmations on the Path" and pick some of those affirmations to use in this exercise.
- ~ Try writing these sentences in your personal journal. You can read them later and notice how your feelings change or don't change about these affirmations of identity.

By acting as if you are the divine, you may stir up feelings for or against the practice. If you stir up feelings of shame, guilt or fear as you affirm your identity with the divine, then that is good information for you on your own path. You may have to examine and perhaps work through some of those feelings so you can succeed with the practice of identification with the divine. If the feelings are overwhelmingly strong, then you either may not be ready for this stage or may even feel that another religious or spiritual understanding would be better for you. I can say this with confidence born out of experience; if you do accept the identification, there can be no better self-image, no more self-confidence and no more love, bliss and joy possible than ensues from engaging in this particular practice.

Try including the affirmation, "As Supreme Awareness, I am the epitome of humility. What I experience myself to be, I also experience everyone and everything to be." Be sure to include some form of this role played identity, since humility or receptivity is an aspect of the Godhead.

As a meditation, a person might continue this into a 30-40 minute sitting, affirming the higher identity throughout as a mantra. In the yoga tradition there are affirmations in Sanskrit that affirm this: "Shivo Ham" (I am one with supreme Shiva), "Aham Brahmasmi" (I am one with Brahman, the creator), "Tat Tvam Asi" (Thou art That) and others. The goal, though, is to carry this supreme identity into your daily life, as well as into your practices. It isn't that a devotee would make a point of this to friends and family; it would be a secret practice that would bring him or her great joy in the midst of living a golden life. No one might even recognize that this practice was going on in the background of their friend or relative's experience, though they might feel the positive effects of them in their friends attitude or countenance.

There is a story my master told more than once about a devotee who was given a supreme mantra by his guru and told he, himself, would achieve enlightenment if he used it. However, he would not achieve enlightenment himself if he gave it to anyone else. The next day, his guru walked by a village center and the devotee was shouting out the mantra to everyone present. The guru scolded him that he would not be able to experience enlightenment this lifetime himself for what he had done. The devotee said to his guru: "Guruji, everyone else here will achieve enlightenment with the mantra. What a small price I will pay for that!"

The feeling of the story suggests that this devotee was forgiven for such a pure motive and did also reach enlightenment. So we may want to keep this practice of supreme identity as a secret practice for ourselves. It may not, by itself alone, take us to paradise, but it will prepare us to accept in the right way the paradise all of our practices and the grace of god elevate us into. Meanwhile, each of our lives and all of the ups and downs will be totally owned by us and nevermore will we identify with ourselves as victims. As THAT we create it all and as THAT we sustain and enjoy it all for a period of time and then as THAT we dissolve it all back into ourselves. As THAT, we hide ourselves in that world, but as THAT we also grace ourselves with the understanding that we are THAT.

Immersion in the Light

MY AIM FOR THIS book was to inspire both NDErs and seekers of all faiths to learn to be drawn closer to pure spirit and even merge with the brilliant Light of Consciousness itself. Seekers who have not had an NDE can learn from NDE experiences how glorious is their goal. Perhaps some NDErs can enliven their NDE experience within them by meditation and they can find themselves living more and more in those higher states of consciousness they experienced during the NDE. Even not-yet-seekers, awakened by some of the content of this book, might explore further within themselves to see if they too have an experience awaiting them just around the corner.

I would like to anticipate some questions that this book might raise in the reader's mind. One might be why the book focuses so much on the nineteen fifties through the seventies. It was in those early decades that Sharyn had her pivitol NDE and in those decades I had childhood experiences, and later, adult awakening experiences. When one is a teenager as Sharyn was, their minds are often focused on everything but their spiritual life. To then have the kind of NDE she did can shake up a person's entire world. And when one believes, as I did at that time, that religions are merely opiate for the masses, and then has the kind of awakenings I shared here, it also turns one's world completely upside down.

Many NDErs report this happening to them. The early experiences, for both Sharyn and myself, being the most dramatic times in our spiritual awakenings, placed those earlier experiences high on my priority list of things to reflect upon and write about. The experience of those three decades easily filled a book, so I ended up not writing about the next 30 some years of dedicated spiritual practices for both of us. Constant work on our spiritual and emotional growth, however, little by little, brought a number of more subtle transformations that would, in fact, take future pages for me to share to an interested public.

Another question that might have reared its head for a reader could be how I know that the experiences Sharyn and other NDErs have are the same as the ones I experienced through meditation. I suppose we will never know. The way she talks about her experiences seems very close to how I speak about mine. Both are larger than life. Both involve an intelligent, loving light, both involve freedom and joy. Both experiences involve communication or communion with a disembodied state of light. Both bring tears of joy to our eyes. It makes some sense that an omnipresent, omniscient, loving and intelligent state of higher consciousness might appear to both those who have clinically died (or became open to it through illness, unconsciousness or spontaneous spiritual awakening) as well as those directly approaching those states through chanting, prayer, meditation and other practices. Because there are levels of subtlety in this higher consciousness, perhaps we will never know if we experience the very same state as someone else. However, this shouldn't keep us from being motivated by each other's shared experience of the same higher being even though our experiences compared to others may be a little like the group of blind men describing the elephant!

I could also imagine a question about the idea I reconfirm that we are one-with that light of consciousness. Some NDErs and some meditators have spoken of the light of consciousness as grace descending upon them as mortal beings. Most of us do pray to it for guidance, for grace, for inspiration and for boons. Some people might argue they would feel pretentious acting as if they were that higher state. Perhaps they picture always being the children of God, but separate from him/her, even after death.

I can only share the experience of my own journey. Along the way over many years, I experienced the shift happen more and more from "I the personality" to "I, as Supreme Awareness." Also in my meditations there was a shift from experiencing only an aching body to experiencing an expanded brilliance as my true identity. I am more apt today to view my life as a "happening", to borrow from the 60's jargon. As "Supreme Awareness", I engage in a day of experiences, in the eternal now, filled with wonder, joy, light, love and happiness, even if, as THAT, I move in and out of heavy heart space or a frustrated gut space or aching body space. It is I, as pure awareness, moving in and out of my own eternal creation of "minor ecstasies" like moods, feelings and bodily distress. Nowadays, I find myself noting to myself, "I sure created a mess here to clean up!", only with a sense of joy over what messes I am free to make and dissolve, knowing as I do by now who I am that does that.

The NDErs, meditators and others who <u>have</u> had the experience of merging and becoming one with the light may be our leaders in this regard. I have identified several stages in my own journey. First I was incredulous that a "poor wretch like me", to quote a line from the hymn *Amazing*

Grace, could be worthy of God's attention. Then came a phase where I understood I was a beloved seeker of the divine, but certainly not "one-with" that higher being. Only later after years of of playing those other roles, did I take serious the higher teachings of my Guru and begin to allow myself to honor those times in meditation where I felt merged and "one-with" The Light. Now, my cutting edge of spiritual growth is to catch any moment where I act as if I am not (or someone else I encounter is not) the highest light and then laugh at my folly. This practice is rewarded by my life dancing in joy around me. My master shared that when he experienced and was willing to own "I AM THAT", into which his master had initiated him, his path opened up to him and greeted him. Perhaps that awaits each and every one of us at some point in our understanding. Perhaps it is a gift of grace that comes when we are devout enough for long enough, as a loving seeker, wanting to know the light.

I want to be sure that the reader understands that I am not representing any one path in writing this book. I am not claiming to be a spokesperson for my Guru's teachings. I think I do justice to the path by writing about my own experiences, but keep in mind that these are my own experiences. This book is not to be considered part any Guru's teaching materials, but rather, is my own effort to continue offering my support as an ordained Spiritual Counselor and teacher of spiritual growth, through my own experiences and studies of divine process.

Thanks to my forty-plus years with my path and my 27 years married to Sharyn (over 30 years of being with her), more and more I feel that there is nowhere to go and only one thing to do. The Eternal-Now has become a constant companion and other things are measured by it, rather than the other way around. If my jewel is always already in my heart, I do not have to seek it or display it. I just recognize my identity with it and secretly radiate it. As Sharyn related in her chapter, I too feel more and more desire to help others reach into their heart to discover that the jewel has always been there too. Pure spirit shows itself more and more, the closer we allow ourselves to be drawn into it. As I allow it to manifest, my life becomes more like it. Gratitude, Gratitude, Gratitude for guidance and transformation.

If I later write about the years following the experiences related here, I hope I will be able to fill in the gaps between wonderful awakenings of spirit as I have shared, and the more ongoing focus on becoming established daily in these magical states of being. There were also traps for me in my early conditioning (and lack of it) that shaped me in ways that seemed to challenge my spiritual growth. Some deeply held dynamics in us may take years of spiritual practice to release. I found that to be true. Ongoing progress on the path may seem less dramatic than early awakenings, but it is the real test of our spiritual character and challenges our karmas that act upon us to create the feeling we are driving with the emergency brake on; a constant drag to becoming established in our highest identity. If I am blessed to write more, it will be about this ongoing effort that is demanded of us by the draw of the light into its wholeness. I hope we may meet again though our communication with one another and many blessings to you who are interested enough to explore what is beckoning you to grow. Om Shanti, Shanti, Shanti.

References

Alexander, E. (2012). *Proof of Heaven: a neurosurgeon's journey into the afterlife.* New York: Simon & Schuster.

Amen, D. G. (2005). *Making a good brain great : The Amen Clinic program for achieving and sustaining optimal mental performance* (1st ed.). New York: Harmony Books.

Armstrong, J., & Armstrong, A.,. (2011). *Awakening the divine within: Kundalini-the gateway to freedom.* [S.l.]: Iuniverse.

Atwater, P. M. H. (2007). *People are dramatically changed by NDEs.* Retrieved from http://www.near-death.com/experiences/evidence05.html

Bohn, D. (1975). *We are not just daffodils.* Santa Clara, California: Volunteers of the Suicide and Crisis Service of Santa Clara County.

Brown, R. ([1958]). *Little flowers of st. francis of assisi* [Fioretti di San Francesco.] (1st complete ed. ed.). Garden City, N.Y.: Hanover House.

Chopra, D., & Greenberg, M. H. (2000). *Deepak Chopra's the angel is near* (St. Martin's Paperbacks ed.). New York, N.Y: St. Martin's Press.

Eddy, Mary Baker (1934). *Science and health with key to the scriptures.* Boston: Christian Science Publishing Society; Reprint edition.

Johnson, Robert A. (1983). *We, understanding the psychology of romantic love.* San Francisco: Harper & Row.

Jones, R. B. (1972). Natural law and psychotherapy. In Grant, J.B. and Welch, R. (Ed.), *Geocentric experience: A bulletin.* Los Gatos, California: Lamplighters Roadway Press.

Jung, C. G. (1963). *Memories, dreams, reflections.* New York: Pantheon Books.

Kipling, R. (1926). *The Works of Rudyard Kipling* (The seven seas edition). Garden City, New York: Doubleday, Page and Co.

Lewis, D. (2005). The physicist as mystic. In J. D. Kenyon (Ed.), *Forbidden history: Extraterrestrial intervention, prehistoric technologies.* [n.p.]: Legendary Times Books.

Long, J., & Perry, P. (2010). Evidence of the afterlife: The science of near-death experiences. New York: HarperOne.

Miller, I. Fear & loathing in the temporal lobes: Correlates of so-called spiritual experiences with sub-clinical epilepsy. Retrieved from http://iona-miller.weebly.com/temporal-lobes.html

Moody, R. A. (1977; 1975). *Life after life :The investigation of a phenom-enon, survival of bodily death.* Boston: G. K. Hall.

Moorjani, Anita (2012). *Dying to be me: My journey from cancer to near death to true healing.* Carlsbad, California: Hay House.

Morse, M., & Perry, P. (1990). *Closer to the light : Learning from chil-dren's near-death experiences* (1st ed.). New York: Villard Books.

Morse, M., & Perry, P. (1992). *Transformed by the light : The powerful effect of near-death experiences on people's lives* (1st ed.). New York, NY: Villard Books.

Muktananda. (1974). *Getting rid of what you haven't got: Talks and con-versations with sri gurudev baba muktananda.* [n.p]: Wordpress.

Patanjali. (1989). *The yoga-sutra of patanjali: A new translation and commentary* (G. Feuerstein Trans.). Rochester, VT: Inner Traditions.

Pearce, J. C. (1971). *The crack in the cosmic egg; challenging constructs of mind and reality.* New York: Julian Press.

Pranavadarshan, P. (2001). *Shri guru gita: The song of the absolute.* San Diego, CA: Pranava.

Ring, K. (1984). *Heading toward omega: In search of the meaning of the near death experience.* New York:William Morrow and Company, Inc.

Ring, K., & Elsaesser Valarino, E. (1998). *Lessons from the light : What we can learn from the near-death experience.* New York: Insight Books.

Flatliners. Schumacher, J., Douglas, M., Bieber, R., Filardi, P., Suther-land, K., Roberts, J., ... Sony Pictures Home Entertainment (Directors). (2007).[Video/DVD] Culver City, Calif: Sony Pictures Home Entertain-ment.

Shakespeare, W. (1996). The complete works of Willliam Shakespeare. Retrieved, from http://www.gutenberg.org

Sutherland, C. (1995, 1993). *Within the light.* New York: Bantam books.

Winkelman, M. (Ed.). (1992). Shamans, priests and witches: A cross-cultural study of magic-religious practitioners. Tempe: Anthropological Research Papers, Arizona State University.

Yogananda, P. (1959 [c1946]). Autobiography of a Yogi. (8th ed.). Los Angeles: Self-Realization Fellowship.